CW00969541

The Cataholic's Handbook

Books by Vernon Coleman include:

The Medicine Men (1975)
Paper Doctors (1976)
Stress Control (1978)
The Home Pharmacy (1980)
Aspirin or Ambulance (1980)
Face Values (1981)
The Good Medicine Guide (1982)
Bodypower (1983)
Thomas Winsden's Cricketing Almanack (1983)
Diary of a Cricket Lover (1984)
Bodysense (1984)
Life Without Tranquillisers (1985)
The Story Of Medicine (1985, 1998)
Mindpower (1986)
Addicts and Addictions (1986)
Dr Vernon Coleman's Guide To Alternative Medicine (1988)
Stress Management Techniques (1988)
Know Yourself (1988)
The Health Scandal (1988)
The 20 Minute Health Check (1989)
Sex For Everyone (1989)
Mind Over Body (1989)
Eat Green Lose Weight (1990)
How To Overcome Toxic Stress (1990)
Why Animal Experiments Must Stop (1991)
The Drugs Myth (1992)
Complete Guide To Sex (1993)
How to Conquer Backache (1993)
How to Conquer Pain (1993)
Betrayal of Trust (1994)
Know Your Drugs (1994, 1997)
Food for Thought (1994, revised edition 2000)
The Traditional Home Doctor (1994)
People Watching (1995)
Relief from IBS (1995)

The Parent's Handbook (1995)
Men in Dresses (1996)
Power over Cancer (1996)
Crossdressing (1996)
How to Conquer Arthritis (1996)
High Blood Pressure (1996)
How To Stop Your Doctor Killing You (1996, revised edition 2003)
Fighting For Animals (1996)
Alice and Other Friends (1996)
Spiritpower (1997)
How To Publish Your Own Book (1999)
How To Relax and Overcome Stress (1999)
Animal Rights – Human Wrongs (1999)
Superbody (1999)
Complete Guide to Life (2000)
Strange But True (2000)
Daily Inspirations (2000)
Stomach Problems: Relief At Last (2001)
How To Overcome Guilt (2001)
How To Live Longer (2001)
Sex (2001)
We Love Cats (2002)
England Our England (2002)
Rogue Nation (2003)
People Push Bottles Up Peaceniks (2003)
The Cats' Own Annual (2003)
Confronting The Global Bully (2004)
Saving England (2004)
Why Everything Is Going To Get Worse Before It Gets Better (2004)
The Secret Lives of Cats (2004)
The Cat Basket (2005)
The Truth They Won't Tell You (And Don't Want You To Know)
     About The EU (2005)
Living in a Fascist Country (2006)
How To Protect and Preserve Your Freedom, Identity and Privacy (2006)
The Cataholic's Handbook (2006)

novels
The Village Cricket Tour (1990)
The Bilbury Chronicles (1992)
Bilbury Grange (1993)
Mrs Caldicot's Cabbage War (1993)
Bilbury Revels (1994)
Deadline (1994)
The Man Who Inherited a Golf Course (1995)
Bilbury Pie (1995)
Bilbury Country (1996)
Second Innings (1999)
Around the Wicket (2000)
It's Never Too Late (2001)
Paris In My Springtime (2002)
Mrs Caldicot's Knickerbocker Glory (2003)
Too Many Clubs And Not Enough Balls (2005)
Tunnel (1980, 2005)

as Edward Vernon
Practice Makes Perfect (1977)
Practise What You Preach (1978)
Getting Into Practice (1979)
Aphrodisiacs – An Owner's Manual (1983)

with Alice
Alice's Diary (1989)
Alice's Adventures (1992)

with Donna Antoinette Coleman
How To Conquer Health Problems Between Ages 50 and 120 (2003)
Health Secrets Doctors Share With Their Families (2005)

The Cataholic's Handbook

by

Vernon Coleman

With illustrations by the author

Chilton Designs

Published by Chilton Designs, Publishing House, Trinity Place, Barnstaple, Devon EX32 9HG, England

This book is copyright. Enquiries should be addressed to the author c/o the publishers.

© Vernon Coleman 2006. The right of Vernon Coleman to be identified as the author of this work has been asserted in accordance with the Copyright, Designs and Patents Act 1988.

ISBN: 1 898146 90 X

All rights reserved. No part may be reproduced, stored in a retrieval system or transmitted, in any form or by any means, electronic, mechanical, photocopying, recording or otherwise without the prior written permission of the author and publisher. This book is sold subject to the condition that it shall not by way of trade or otherwise be lent, re-sold, hired out or otherwise circulated without the publisher's prior consent in any form of binding or cover other than that in which it is published.

A catalogue record for this book is available from the British Library.

Printed by Antony Rowe Limited, Wiltshire

Contents List

Dedication

Cats are God's treat to all Uprights, says Donna Antoinette. And what a variety of treats he has given us. A never-ending parade of colours and personalities. Without cats life would be so much poorer and the world would be a considerably duller place. If we pass a cat in the street Donna Antoinette always smiles and says that God has treated her kindly that day. And so this book is dedicated, with my love as always, to Donna Antoinette, always a playful kitten, never a sleepy cat. It is also dedicated, with respect and real affection, to all stray cats, all cats in vivisection laboratories and all cats who do not have an Upright whose love they can call their own.

Vernon Coleman March 2006

P.S. As readers of my seven other cat books will already know I use the word 'Upright' instead of the phrase 'human being'. The word was first used in this way by Alice in her two books *Alice's Diary* and *Alice's Adventures* and I have adopted it and used it, in her memory, ever since.

Chapter One

How Well Have You Been Trained By Your Cat?

Do you own your cat, or does your cat own you? It's a tricky question. But if you work your way through this quiz then you should, by the time you get to the end of it, have some sort of an answer.

1. Do you get up in the morning:
a)   when you want to get up
b)   when your cat wants you to get up

2. At Christmas do you:
a)   buy your cat a present
b)   put the cat's name on the cards you send to other people
c)   both a) and b)
d)   neither a) nor b)

3. On your cat's birthday do you:
a)   buy him or her a special treat and/or sing Happy Purrthday
b)   take no notice of the occasion whatsoever

4. Do you feed your cat:
a)   before you eat because he comes first
b)   before you eat so that he won't be a nuisance
c)   after you eat however much fuss he makes

5. If your cat doesn't like the food you give him/her do you:
a)   just keep re-offering the same food until he eats it or goes out and catches something
b)   rummage around in the cupboard and open something else
c)   get dressed, get the car out and drive 15 miles to buy something you are confident will prove acceptable

6. If a friend treated their child the way that you treat your cat would you say they were:
a)   a good parent
b)   spoiling it rotten
c)   cruel

7. If your cat was missing how soon would you start worrying:
a)   never
b)   after one hour
c)   after 30 minutes
d)   after 30 seconds, if you could hold out that long

8. Who has most toys:
a)   you
b)   your cat
c)   next door's children

9. You are getting ready to go out. You find the cat asleep on something you intended to wear. Do you:
a)   move the cat
b)   wear something else

10. What does your cat do when his dishes need to be washed up:
a)   stay asleep in his basket
b)   stay asleep on the sofa
c)   jump up and help do the dishes

11. If your cat decides to sit on your lap do you:
a)   feel thrilled, delighted and grateful and keep very still so that he is comfortable
b)   throw him or her off

12. How often have you sat on your cat's lap:
a)   never
b)   just the once

Now check your score:
   1. a) 1 b) 2
   2. a) 2 b) 2 c) 4 d) 1
   3. a) 2 b) 1
   4. a) 3 b) 2 c) 1
   5. a) 1 b) 2 c) 3
   6. a) 2 b) 3 c) 1
   7. a) 1 b) 2 c) 3 d) 4
   8. a) 1 b) 2 c) 1
   9. a) 1 b) 4
   10. a) 3 b) 3 c) 1
   11. a) 2 b) 1
   12. a) 2 b) 1

What do your results mean?

♦   If you scored 15 or less then you have managed to stay in charge. You're the boss and the cat knows it.

♦   If you scored 16 to 22 you are fighting a battle for supremacy. But things don't look good. Do this questionnaire again in twelve months' time and you'll probably find that your score is higher.

♦   If you scored 23 or more then your cat is in charge. You know it. And, more importantly, the cat knows it.

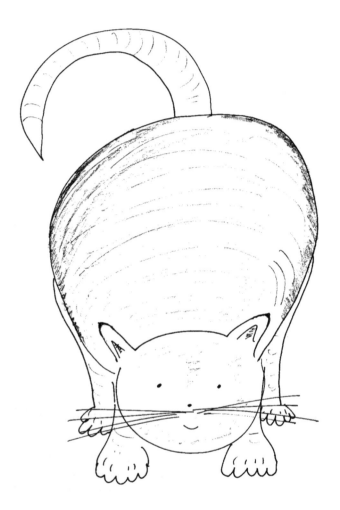

The Pounce

Chapter Two

Thirty Simple Ways To Make Sure Your Cat Loves You For Ever

1. To understand the relationship between cats and Uprights properly you need to know one thing: you don't own your cat. Your cat owns you. It is a nonsense to describe the Upright who feeds and cares for a cat as an owner. Uprights no more 'own' cats than they own the sun or the moon. In a relationship between a cat and an Upright the only creature legitimately entitled to the title 'owner' is the one with four legs and a tail.

2. Let your cat train you. Don't fight it. Life will be easier and far more pleasant if you just give in and let your cat run things. Your cat knows what it wants. Just do it

3. Do not expect a lie-in on Saturday or Sunday mornings. Cats do not recognise weekends. Why should they – they never go to work. Every day is play day.

4. Cats like beds. Preferably your bed. It doesn't matter how much you spend on buying a special cat basket (even if it has feather soft cushions and under-mattress electric heating) your cat will always prefer your bed. However, cats are invariably generous and your cat will probably allow you to share the bed. As long as you stick to one edge.

5. Do not put your cat out at night. If you do then all through the next day you will find the carpet outside the bathroom door littered

with tiny corpses (or worse still, the entrails from tiny corpses). Why do you think your cat does this? Think about it. Would you like to be thrown out into the cold and wet every night?

6. You must supply your cat with a scratching post so that it can keep its claws nicely shaped. Your cat will not, of course, use a scratching post (it will much prefer to use an item of furniture – preferably the one decent item of furniture in the house) but it will be offended if you do not at least make the effort and provide one.

7. There is only one type of litter to buy: the best, the finest, purest, litter you can buy. It should be horrendously, hideously, unbelievably expensive and preferably made from ground hand picked pearls mixed with hand sifted Arabian sand. Never switch. Cats dislike a change in their little tray contents just as much they dislike a change in their food. (The only exception to this is if a more expensive brand becomes available.)

8. If your cat has difficulty in seeing, make sure that you leave furniture exactly where it is. And do not buy any new furniture either. If your cat is hard of hearing use hand signals or a torch to let it know when food is being prepared. (Though remember that some deaf cats can hear the vibration of a tin being opened.)

9. Make sure that you clip your cat's claws regularly. This is not something a cat should be left to do all by itself. Can you really imagine your cat operating a pair of nail clippers? Exactly.

10. Catering is a crucial part of any good cat-Upright relationship. Make sure that you vary the menu but also take care that you do not give your cat anything he or she doesn't like, isn't used to and hasn't had before. When shopping for cat food there is one simple rule to remember: buy the most expensive food available. It is important to remember how crucial price can be. If your local store is selling a favourite brand of cat food at a reduced price ask the assistant if you can pay full price. Food bought at a discount will not be eaten.

11. Cats like to be able to move around the house freely and without their progress being interrupted by unexpected, loud noises. To help make life more comfortable for your cat make sure that you do not put vases or other delicate objects on jumping or landing points on mantelpieces or pieces of furniture.

12. Cats don't like tap water. They don't know where it's been, it tastes of chemicals, it contains old drugs and, most important of all, it's so cheap that it's almost free. Cats prefer bottled water. (There are only two exceptions to this: although cats won't drink tap water that has been put into a bowl, they will drink tap water as it drips straight from the tap. And they will drink it from the toilet bowl.) If your cat doesn't seem to be drinking enough, try flavouring his or her drinking water with fish or meat juice.

13. Never close doors. If you close a door a cat will always want to be on the other side. To a cat, a closed door is a sign of a closed mind.

14. If your cat seems under the weather try feeding him tinned sardines or pilchards in tomato sauce. These will work best if fed by hand.

15. Make sure that you brush your cat regularly to prevent hairballs developing. This will save your cat the effort of licking itself. You will benefit from this because you will be far less likely to step into a puddle of hairy sick as you head for the bathroom in the middle of the night.

16. Remember your cat in your will. Make arrangements for a friend to look after him or her if anything should happen to you – and leave plenty of money to pay for food, water and other essentials. Few things are sadder than the postcards seen in animal charity shop windows which advertise the fact that 15-year-old Kitty is now homeless because her Upright has died. Don't expose your cat to such humiliation.

17. Put a bird table outside your living room window so that your cat has something entertaining to watch when it is raining. Build a small platform out of cushions so that your cat can see out of the

window. If necessary, hire expensive (but quiet and cat-friendly) workmen to build a framework on which to place the cushions.

18. We all have secret storage places where we put important things for safe-keeping. Your cat will probably store many of its most valuable items (toys, bits of food, half-eaten mice, lizard tails and so on) under the fridge. Remember this when you move house. All these items should be transported carefully to your new home and put back underneath the fridge.

19. Ignore the textbooks and the alleged experts who will tell you that cats should be fed sparingly and as little as two or three times a day. Cats should be fed whenever they want to be fed. Your cat will tell you when it's meal time. Listen and obey.

20. It is easy to teach a cat tricks. It is even possible to teach an old cat new tricks. There are two ways to do this. First, wait until your cat does what you want it to do. Then reward it and claim the credit. Alternatively, when your cat has done something really clever, reward it. Pretend that what it did was what you wanted it to do. And claim the credit.

21. You should provide at least one litter tray per cat. Clean the tray at least three times a day. Provide the litter tray with a cover and leave it in the same place all the time. Do not move the tray, this will cause confusion. (How would you like it, if you got up in the middle of the night to go to the toilet and discovered that the toilet had become a pouffe?) All cats (even cats which have the freedom to go out into the garden) will need to have a litter tray available. It is unreasonable to expect a cat to go outside to use nature's facilities when the weather is inclement or the ground is damp.

22. If your cat's bottom sticks over the edge of its litter tray (with predictably damaging consequences for the carpet), put the tray into a larger tray. It is unreasonable and impractical to expect your cat to alter the position of its bottom.

23. If your cat has an 'accident' indoors, make sure that you clean up

with biological washing liquid rather than an ammonia based cleaner. A cat is likely to regard an ammonia based cleaner as competition.

24. If you acquire a new partner who doesn't like cats you will have to give up the new partner. Try to break the news gently and make sure that the redundant partner does not have any opportunity to throw things at the cat.

25. If other cats bully your cat you are well within your rights to defend your cat. Under the Geneva Convention (Cats) it is permissible to use a water pistol to make your point clear.

26. Don't let strange dogs or cats walk around where they can be seen by your cat. Such exhibitions may be regarded as provocative and disturbing by your cat.

27. Elderly cats sleep 75% of the time, though naturally very little of this sleeping is done at night. Make sure that you tiptoe around the house. Try to make sure that neighbours and workmen do not make too much noise while your cat is sleeping.

28. If your cat has difficulty getting onto your favourite chair build it a ramp. You can do this by placing your favourite cushions and pillows in a heap.

29. Cats like a massage at least once an hour. A massage should last around five minutes and should involve gentle kneading of the back and the neck regions.

30. If you want your cat to be able to travel by car, make sure that you get it used to cars by driving it around when it is still a kitten. Please make sure, however, that the car in which the cat travels is a luxury model. Cats do not like travelling in down-market vehicles. More importantly, they do not like to be *seen* travelling in down-market vehicles.

For the Tilsdales, shopping was a real family affair.

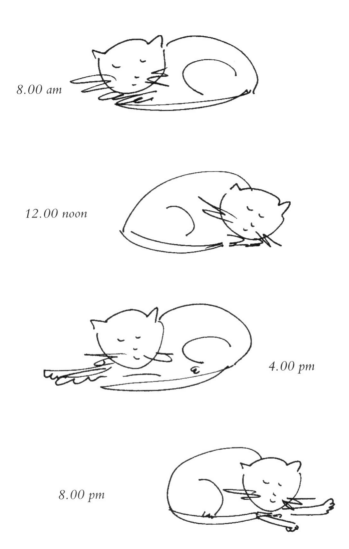

8.00 am

12.00 noon

4.00 pm

8.00 pm

Tiddles has a busy day

Chapter Three

Favourite Proverbs Concerning Cats

I have produced lists of proverbs in some of my previous cat books. But I am constantly encountering more – it seems that every country in the world has its own collection of native proverbs. Here is another collection of astonishing proverbs relating to cats. Some of these were sent to me by readers around the world. Others were collected from mewspapers and mogazines.

1. 'Who doesn't feed the cat feeds the mice.' (Serbia)

2. 'The cat who scratches, scratches for himself.' (Russia)

3. 'He who denies the cat skimmed milk must give the mouse cream.' (Russia)

4. 'A lame cat is better than a swift horse when rats infest the palace.' (China)

5. 'A blind cat catches only a dead rat.' (China)

6. 'The cat that does not catch mice, and the man who does not like to talk, will both go hungry.' (Czechoslovakia – now Czech Republic)

7. 'A house without either a cat or a dog is the house of a scoundrel.' (Portugal)

8. 'The man who goes to law often loses an ox to win a cat.' (Romania)

9. 'The cat knows whose lips she licks.' (Italy)

10. 'The cat who frightens the mice away is as good as the cat who eats them.' (Germany)

11. 'Happy owner, happy cat. Indifferent owner, reclusive cat.' (China)

12. 'When you have trodden on the cat, what help is it to stroke her back?' (Switzerland)

13. 'The cat who failed to reach the sausage hanging from the ceiling said: 'It is not worth the trouble; today is Friday.' (Russia)

14. 'The cat failed to make off with the liver and said: 'I am fasting today.' (Turkey)

15. 'The cat who could not reach the roast cried: 'In honour of my father's memory, I will not eat it.' (Kurdistan)

16. 'Who can forbid to a cat the top of the oven, or a boy to a girl.' (Livonia)

17. 'A timid cat makes a bold mouse.' (Scotland)

18. 'Whoever has never seen a tiger, let him look at a cat, and whoever has never seen a robber, let him look at a butcher.' (India)

19. 'It is a brave bird that makes its nest in the cat's ear.' (India)

20. 'Go like a dog; come like the cat.' (India)

21. 'The cat dreams of garbage.' (India)

22. 'The cat laps the moonbeams in the bowl of water, thinking them to be milk.' (India)

23. 'To live long, eat like a cat, drink like a dog.' (Germany)

24. 'Cats are everywhere at home where one feeds them.' (Germany)

25. 'Even mice may bite dead cats.' (Germany)

26. 'Cats and women are said to have been made on the same day.' (Germany)

27. 'The cat loves fish, but hates wet feet.' (Italy)

28. 'Old cats mean young mice.' (Italy)

29. 'Who saves, saves for the cat.' (Italy)

30. 'An old cat will not burn himself.' (Ireland)

31. 'If the cat had a churn, her paw would often be in it.' (Ireland)

32. 'You won't get a cat but its skin.' (Ireland)

33. 'House without hound, cat, or child, house without love or affection.' (Ireland)

34. 'What would a young cat do but eat mice?' (Ireland)

35. 'She would drink the cream and say the cat was an old rogue.' (Ireland)

36. 'It is for her own good that the cat purrs.' (Ireland)

37. 'She wipes the plate with the cat's tail.' (Ireland)

38. 'The four fortunes of the cat: the housewife's error, walking without care, no water in milk and sight at night as well as by day.' (Ireland)

39. 'The three most pleasant things: a cat's kitten, a goat's kid and a young widow-woman.' (Ireland)

40. 'Three pairs that never agree: two married women in the same house, two cats with one mouse, and two bachelors after one young woman.' (Ireland)

41. 'The cat's a saint when there are no mice around.' (Japan)

42. 'The borrowed cat catches no mice.' (Japan)

43. 'When the cat mourns the mouse, don't take her seriously.' (Japan)

44. 'Whenever a rat teases a cat, he is leaning against a hole.' (Liberia)

45. 'It takes a good many mice to kill a cat.' (Denmark)

46. 'A cat is a lion to a mouse.' (Albania)

47. 'A cat that is always crying catches no mice.' (Arabia)

48. 'A cat bitten once by a snake dreads even rope.' (Arabia)

49. 'A scalded cat dreads even cold water.' (France)

50. 'If you do not rear cats, you will raise mice.' (Bulgaria)

51. 'Those who don't like cats won't get handsome mates.' (Holland)

52. 'A cat which mews loudly catches few mice.' (Holland)

53. 'For the sake of the grease, the cat licks the candlestick.' (Holland)

54. 'A cat that is locked up may change into a lion.' (Holland)

55. 'During the cat's harvest hens are deaf.' (Holland)

56. 'It's a bad thing to buy a cat in a bag.' (France)

57. 'A cat has nine lives. For three he plays, for three he strays, and for the last three he stays.' (England)

58. 'A good cat deserves a good rat.' (France)

59. 'The greedy cat makes the servant girl watchful.' (France)

60. 'Singing cats and whistling girls will come to a bad end.' (England)

61. 'Though the cat winks a while, yet sure he is not blind.' (England)

62. 'A cat with a straw tail keeps away from the fire.' (England)

Tiddles and Tiddlelina listened intently while Gordon told them (at great length) about his adventures in next door's garden.

63. 'A cat always eats fish from the tail.' (Estonia)

64. 'He who is a little cat outside is a little dog at home.' (Estonia)

65. 'A dog's tongue has nine healings; a cat's claw has snake's poison.' (Estonia)

66. 'A girl without a needle is like a cat without a claw.' (Estonia)

67. 'When cat and mouse agree, the farmer has no chance.' (England)

68. 'Better be the head of a cat than the tail of a lion.' (England)

69. 'The cat shuts its eyes when it steals cream.' (England)

70. 'Whoever keeps a black cat will prosper and grow fat.' (England)

71. 'If all the cats in the house are black, lasses have no lack of lovers.' (England)

Nelson's cat

Chapter Four

A Compilation Of 229 Strange And Curious Facts About Cats

Cat Fact 1

Each nipple on a lactating mother cat has its own smell and as a result the kittens in a litter each become attached to one particular nipple. When I mentioned this to a friend who plays cricket twice a week during the summer he looked at me knowingly. 'You mean that each kitten has its own personal nipple?' he asked. I agreed that this was what I meant. 'It's the same in our changing room,' said my friend. 'Everyone in our team has a favourite coat hook.'

Cat Fact 2

Marilyn Monroe, the legendary film star, had a Persian cat called Mitsou. She once complained that she had tried to call a vet for her cat but had found it quite impossible. 'They think I'm kidding when I say: 'This is Marilyn Monroe. My cat's having kittens,' she said. 'They think I'm some kind of nut and hang up.'

Cat Fact 3

The largest litter in history was produced by an English female Burmese cat called Tarawood Antigone. In August 1970, when she was four-years-old, Tarawood Antigone gave birth to 19 kittens. The kittens were delivered by Caesarian section. Sadly, four of the kittens were stillborn and of the survivors all but one were male. How would you fancy having 15 kittens climbing everywhere? (Yes, I know, you'd love it.)

Cat Fact 4

A Maine Coon cat called Leo, who lived in Chicago, Illinois measured 48 inches from his nose to the tip of his tail. That is a lot of cat and would, stretched out, require two full sized laps. Leo was (and probably still is) the longest cat in the world.

Cat Fact 5

Mike, who was the British Museum's official cat from 1909 to 1929, was said to prefer sole to whiting and whiting to haddock. He liked sardines but didn't much like herring. He didn't like cod at all. I think it is nice that someone noticed these idiosyncrasies and even nicer that someone bothered to write them down.

Mike was said to prefer sole to whiting and whiting to haddock.

Cat Fact 6

It is a myth that a falling cat will always survive because it will land on its feet. A falling cat will twist in the air so that it lands feet first but cats who fall from high places are, nevertheless, often injured or killed. When cats fall they stand a better chance of surviving if the fall is of around eight storeys. Once a cat has reached its terminal velocity or greatest speed (which it does after falling five storeys) it can spread its limbs and relax and be in a better position to absorb the impact when it hits the ground. A cat called Andy who lived with Florida senator Ken Myer, once survived a fall of 16 storeys (this definitely left the politician's cat with just eight lives) but the record for falling out of a high building is said to be held by a cat who fell 46 storeys and survived.

The record for falling out of a high building is said to be held by a cat who fell 46 storeys and survived.

Cat Fact 7

Cats like upholstered and fabric-covered furniture better than smooth or shiny stuff.

Cat Fact 8

The smallest cat in history was a fully-grown male blue-point Himalayan Persian called Tinker Toy. The diminutive Tinker Toy was 2.75 inches tall and 7.5 inches long. Oddly enough Tinker Toy lived in the same American State as the longest cat in the world – Illinois, USA.

Cat Fact 9

The French impressionist painter Pierre-Auguste Renoir is probably best known for his paintings of naked, and usually fairly well-upholstered, young women. (He was, according to art critics, particularly good at illustrating 'the luminosity of a young woman's skin in the outdoors'.) However, observers of Renoir's paintings will notice that the painter put many fine cats into his paintings. The cats were usually sat alongside or on the lap of the woman Renoir was painting. I have it on good authority that the painter Degas was a great fan of Renoir's cats. Well-known paintings by Renoir include: *Sleeping With A Cat* and *Julie Manet With A Cat*.

Cat Fact 10

An American cat called Furball is reputed to have the longest tail of any cat in the world. In March 2001, Furball's tail was measured at 16 inches.

Cat Fact 11

The Paris home of the Swiss painter Theophile Alexandre Steinlen was regarded as a shrine to cats and was known around town as 'Cats' Corner'.

Cat Fact 12

When cats hunt mice it is generally considered (by people and cats who know about these things) that an average of one pounce in every three results in success. Even the very best mousers can only do slightly better than this.

Cat Fact 13

In the 1930's a man who was brought before the Marylebone magistrates accused of having deserted his wife offered as a defence the fact that his wife lived for her cat, had sat up for seven nights nursing it and had fed it on a diet of fillet steak and meat extract. The implication was that this level of devotion to a cat was a sound reason for ending the marriage. The man should have been horse-whipped but, sadly, there is no record of this having happened.

Cat Fact 14

Edward Lowe invented cat litter in 1947. He invented it to help out a neighbour who was fed up of the mess caused by using ashes in a cat tray. In 1990, Mr Lowe sold his business for £110 million, proving, yet again, the truth of the old adage: 'Where there's muck there's brass'.

Cat Fact 15

In the 70 years between 1930 and 2000 the life expectancy of the domestic cat doubled from 8 to 16 years.

Cat Fact 16

The British poet T. S. Eliot said that cats should have three names: an everyday one, something rather more grand and then the name that the cat has for himself. So, for example, you might call your cat Sooty on weekdays and His Lordship The Chief High Executioner Charles Fitzgerald Windsor on Sundays and feast days. The name that Sooty has for himself will, of course, be a secret.

Cat Fact 17

There are some reports circulating that cat racing used to be a popular spectator sport in England. Some historians claim that the first official cat race track was opened in Dorset in 1936 and that the cat racing seen there was similar in format to greyhound racing. Cats were said to have chased an electric mouse round and round a track. I have my doubts about the truth of this piece of history. No cat worth its fish would be stupid enough to chase an electric mouse. However, other historians claim that cat racing can be traced back much further and that it was popular in northern English towns for some years in the late 19th century. A cat called Marmy was reputed to have won over £20,000 guineas for its owner. In those races cats were released at one end of a field and expected to run to the other end of the field when called. It is reputed that Marmy was fed only on fresh salmon. There has been no report of cat racing in England since the early 1950's though occasionally there are still rumours of cat racing in Northern Scotland and in the more rural parts of New Zealand.

Cat racing used to be a popular spectator sport in England

Cat Fact 18

Erwin Schrodinger, a Nobel Prize winning physicist and philosopher (renowned for helping to establish the mathematics of quantum mechanics) created a dilemma known as 'Schrodinger's Cat'. This says that if we observe something we may, by our observing, change what happens and therefore destroy the validity of our observations. For example, if we put a cat into a box and cover the box we can't be sure what the cat is doing. But as soon as we remove the lid and look in we disturb the cat and change its behaviour. You and I might think this sounds pretty obvious and hardly the sort of observation requiring a brain which needs covering with a size seven and three quarters hat, but Schrodinger had a Nobel Prize sitting on his mantelpiece so what do you and I know?

Cat Fact 19

There is no doubt that cats are not just sentient creatures but are also generous and kindly. There are many stories of cats who have helped injured or endangered Uprights, risking their own lives to protect the people with whom they live. There are also numerous stories of cats awakening households to warn of a fire.

Cat Fact 20

A domesticated tomcat becomes sexually active around its first birthday. Rather surprisingly, wild tomcats don't become sexually mature until three to six months later.

Cat Fact 21

An American computer programmer is said to have developed a computer program called PawSense which detects when a cat is walking on the keys. The computer then makes a noise which encourages the cat to go somewhere else. Just how a computer can differentiate between the random key bashing of a wandering cat and the almost equally random key bashing of the average author is something of a mystery.

Cat Fact 22

The domestic cat is the only species of cat able to hold its tail vertical while walking. Pretty impressive, eh?

Cat Fact 23

A female tortoiseshell cat called Towser, who lived at the Glenturret distillery in Scotland, is reported to have killed at least three mice a day throughout her adult life. She was 24 when she died and is credited with having killed 30,000 mice though I have no idea who kept count or why.

Cat Fact 24

Cats are blamed for the fact that there are fewer birds around in our gardens these days. This is unfair. Cats do not catch many birds. Cats will go after anything that moves but being intrinsically lazy creatures they will choose to go after the easiest prey. And so the prey of choice is usually a rodent (none of which can fly) rather than a bird (most of which can). Wild animals catch far more birds than cats do but humans are the birds' worst enemies. We kill birds by destroying their habitat and using pesticides on gardens and farmland.

Cat Fact 25

Scientific evidence suggests that cats prefer adults to children. Children are too abrupt, too noisy and too unpredictable to suit cats.

Cat Fact 26

When a cat is frightened it will endeavour to disguise this fact by attempting to look bored. Cats can look bored (and disdainful) better than any other creature on earth.

Cat Fact 27

Small cats can purr while breathing out and while breathing in. Big cats, such as lions and tigers, can purr only when breathing out. So, if you are stuck in a room in the dark with a cat, you should be able to identify the size of the cat by listening to its purring. This knowledge could save your life and so obviously this one fact alone makes this book a valuable addition to your library.

Cat Fact 28
Queen Victoria had a cat named White Heather which died at Buckingham Palace during the reign of Edward VII.

Cat Fact 29
When he was Governor of California, Ronald Reagan (later to become President Reagan) signed a bill which limited the freedom with which people in California could kick cats.

Cat Fact 30
If you are trying to hold a cat who doesn't want to be held, try to be gentle (but firm). If you are rough with a cat it will struggle more.

Cat Fact 31
Horace Walpole, the English writer, made a grand tour of Europe in 1747. While he was away his cat Selima, described both as a tortoiseshell and a tabby, drowned in what is sometimes referred to as a goldfish bowl but was probably a goldfish pond. To commemorate this sad event Walpole's chum, Thomas Gray (famous for his *Elegy Written in a Country Churchyard*) who had accompanied Walpole on his tour and who had a way with long self-explanatory titles, wrote a poem entitled *Ode on the Death of a Favourite Cat Drowned in a Tub of Gold Fishes*. It was this poem which gave us the phrase 'All that glitters is not gold'.

Cat Fact 32
Uprights sleep about one third of their time. Cats sleep two thirds of their lives. It is fortunate that Uprights and cats do some of their sleeping at the same time.

Cat Fact 33
It was the Romans (who kept cats to keep their granaries free of rodents) who first brought cats to Britain. So, three cheers for the Romans, please.

Cat Fact 34

During the Middle Ages citizens throughout Europe got into the habit of putting ceramic cats onto their roofs to ward off evil spirits. In France, where houses tend to be left alone a good deal, and where restorations are usually only considered after something has fallen down, houses can still be seen which have ceramic cats sitting on their roofs.

Cat Fact 35

When a cat rubs against you with its head it is marking you with the scent glands at the corner of its mouth. Cats who are allowed out of the house tend to mark their Uprights more often and more vigorously than cats who are confined indoors. Cats who are the only cat in a household tend to rub and mark their Uprights more often than cats who have to share an Upright with other cats.

Cat Fact 36

Sir Walter Scott didn't like cats when he was a young man. He was, in short, a Wally. When he grew up into a fully-fledged Upright, Scott apologised for his previous lack of appreciation and generally made it pretty clear that he thought that cats were terribly fine creatures. He then stopped being a Wally and became a Walter again.

Cat Fact 37

The English poet Thomas Hood had a cat called Tabitha Longclaws Tiddleywink. Tabitha had a kitten called Scratchaway. I mention this only because these are such beautiful names.

Cat Fact 38

Cats often prefer to scratch on their owner's favourite chair rather than a special scratching post. This is not through any sense of mischief but is because the cat can smell its owner on the chair and is adding its scent to the mixture (cats have scent glands underneath their front paws). So, when a cat scratches your favourite chair you can, and should, regard the scratch marks as signs of affection.

Cat Fact 39

Give or take an inch or two, most cats are roughly the same size – unlike dogs which can vary in size down to a Chihuahua and up to a Great Dane or St. Bernard.

Cat Fact 40

Drug tests done on animals can produce dangerously misleading information. Thalidomide safely passed tests on animals. Morphine calms people but has the opposite effect when given to cats. Penicillin and aspirin both kill cats. Digitalis is so toxic to animals that it would have never been cleared for Uprights, but it remains our most useful heart drug.

Cat Fact 41

Although the first recorded cat show took place at the St. Giles Fair in Winchester, England in 1598, the first major cat show took place in 1871 at the Crystal Palace in London and it was then that cats were given classes and standards. The show at Crystal Palace was organised by a Mr Harrison Weir who, with his brothers, made up the judges. One of Mr Weir's cats did quite well in the judging. The show was organised to combat the sinister reputation that cats had at the time.

Cat Fact 42

Balinese cats are also known as long-haired Siamese cats. Not surprisingly, long-haired Siamese cats are also known as Balinese cats.

Cat Fact 43

Cat skin is relatively insensitive to temperature change. Uprights will yelp if their skin touches anything at 112 F or above but cats won't even start to feel uncomfortable until they touch something at 124 F. When I was a small boy I shared life with a cat called Timmy who frequently sat far too close to our electric fire. I'll never forget the smell of singed fur.

Cat Fact 44

A cat's sense of smell is very important. A cat uses its sense of smell to find food and to decide whether or not to eat it. Cats won't eat what they can't smell. Cats go off their food when they are ill because their ability to smell has gone – and it is their sense of smell which stimulates their appetite. Canned food that has dried out and doesn't smell won't be attractive to a cat.

Cat Fact 45

A cat's top speed is around 30 m.p.h.. This is about the same sort of pace as can be achieved by a grizzly bear, a racehorse, a warthog, a white-tailed deer and a white rhino.

Cat Fact 46

According to the ancient *Book of Lismore* (a collection of Irish legends about saints) three young clergymen decided to sail the seas and spread the Gospel. As a sign of their faith they agree to take three loaves with them – and nothing else. At the last minute the youngest of the three changed his mind. 'I'll take the little cat, after all,' he announced.

Cat Fact 47

Cats don't like being stared at; they regard it as threatening. They probably also consider it rather rude – unless, of course, you are only staring to admire.

Cat Fact 48

Cats recognise and share their owner's suffering. If an Upright is under a great deal of stress, then any cats who live in the same home will feel stressed too. A stressed out cat will lick itself so much that it pulls out its fur.

Cat Fact 49

Aldous Huxley advised a prospective young writer to buy lots of paper, pen and ink and two cats. These, he insisted, were the essentials for a writer's life.

Cat Fact 50

You can tell a good deal about what a cat is thinking from the way it holds its tail. For example:

- A tail held up straight means that the tail's owner is really pleased to see you.

- If a tail curves gently down and then up again at the tip it means that the cat is feeling relaxed.

- When a tail is slightly raised and softly curved it suggests that the cat is interested in something.

- If a female cat's tail is on one side this is a 'come on' to tomcats. It means: 'Let's make love'.

- When a tail is lowered and fluffed out it denotes a pretty unhappy pussy.

- A cat who holds its tail fairly upright and still, but with a twitching tip is feeling irritated.

- When a cat holds its tail straight up and fully bristled it is feeling rather aggressive. Watch out!

- If a cat's tail is swishing from side to side it suggests that the tail's owner is about to attack.

- When a cat's tail is still, but has a rapidly twitching tip, it is a sign that the cat is about to attack.

A tail held up straight means that the tail's owner is really pleased to see you

Cat Fact 51

According to Parisian professor Alphonse Leon Grimaldi, cats have a language of about six hundred words. You will not be in the slightest bit surprised to hear that cats have far more words in their vocabulary than dogs.

Cat Fact 52

Cats can taste sweet things but they don't like them as much as Uprights tend to do. Chocolate is toxic to cats (especially dark chocolate) and can prove fatal. Cats prefer bitter or salty tasting foods. Of course, cats don't always take much notice of what the experts say. I once lived with a cat called Alice who hated fish and loved chocolate. I didn't know, when I gave it to her, that it might prove toxic to her and I have to admit that it never seemed to do her any harm.

Cat Fact 53

During the 6th century BC many Greeks kept cats as curiosities and allowed them to live lives of idle luxury. The Greeks did not expect their cats to work for a living by catching mice. They kept polecats or ferrets to do the dirty work. The cats were expected to loll around, look beautiful, take catnaps and nibble on delicacies.

Cat Fact 54

Like Uprights, cats get two sets of teeth. The first or deciduous teeth come between 4th and 6th week and are replaced between 15th and 17th week. By the time a kitten is seven months old it should have all its adult teeth.

Cat Fact 55

Cats like it when Uprights talk on the telephone. They think that the person who is talking is talking to them. (What possible other explanation could there be for an apparently sentient, living creature talking into a piece of plastic?)

Cat Fact 56

The cat was the only animal allowed into ancient Roman temples.

Cat Fact 57

In the 6th century, when Buddhism was introduced into Japan, it was customary for the Buddhists to keep at least two cats in each temple to protect the manuscripts from being nibbled by mice.

Cat Fact 58

Toads are dangerous to cats because they have warts which contain a poison called bufotalin.

Cat Fact 59

Tortoiseshell cats have fur in a mixture of black, orange and white. Almost all tortoiseshell cats are female. The few male tortoiseshell cats which exist are usually infertile.

Cat Fact 60

Here's a list of some of the strangest foods enjoyed by cats:

1. Whisky and water

2. Curry

3. Peas

4. Broad beans

5. Almond biscuits

6. Roquefort cheese

7. Dark chocolate

8. Spaghetti

9. Christmas cake

10. Tomato soup

(I don't mean that the foods are strange but that it is, perhaps, rather strange that cats should like them.)

Cat Fact 61

In France cat lovers are so ardent that they are known as 'félinophiles enragés'.

Cat Fact 62

An American company has produced a series of television shows made especially for cats. The shows feature birds, squirrels and bouncing balls and are probably much more entertaining and considerably more educational than anything made by broadcasters making programmes for Uprights.

Cat Fact 63

Male cats are called 'tomcats' because of a story called *The Life And Adventures Of A Cat* which was published in 1760. In the story a ram cat (the then current name for male cats) was called Tom.

Cat Fact 64

A cat's tongue feels like sandpaper because it contains lots of little hook-like papillae which help the cat clean its fur and lick the flesh from the bones of its prey. The cat's tongue really is an effective tool for stripping flesh from bones. So, if you let a cat lick your finger long enough it will eventually get down to bone. I am told (and am prepared to take someone else's word for it) that big cats such as tigers and lions have tongues which are much rougher.

Cat Fact 65

In the middle of the 10th century, Howell the Good of Wales introduced a piece of legal code which fixed the value of a ratting cat, and the penalties for endangering its life, wounding it or not caring for it properly. A champion ratter was considered by dear old Howell (or his advisers) to be as valuable as a six-month-old calf or a completely weaned pig.

Cat Fact 66

The cat, the camel and the giraffe have something in common. They all walk the same way – alternating between using the front and hind legs on one side and then the front and hind legs of the other side. All other animals move their left front leg and their right back leg and then their right front leg and their left back leg.

Cat Fact 67

There are thousands of stamps available which carry pictures of cats. The first stamp to carry a picture of a cat was published in Germany in 1887. The stamp showed a cat with a fish in its mouth. There is a British set of stamps illustrating the Rudyard Kipling Just So story *The Cat That Walked By Himself*. A Spanish stamp which commemorates Charles Lindbergh's record breaking flight from New York to Paris in 1927 shows Lindbergh's cat Patsy watching Lindbergh's plane take off. (Patsy normally accompanied Lindbergh on his flights but Lindbergh felt that the first transatlantic flight was too dangerous. He may have also been unable to decide where to put the litter tray.)

Cat Fact 68

Here is a list of twelve countries which have each issued more than ten different stamps carrying beautiful pictures of adorable cats:

1. S Tome e Principe
2. Republica de Guinea Ecuatorial
3. Royaume du Cambodge
4. Republique du Benin
5. DPR Korea
6. Guine Bissau
7. Republique du Congo
8. Cuba
9. Vietnam
10. Lao
11. Afghanistan
12. Mongolia

Cat Fact 69

Cats can predict earthquakes. When an earthquake is coming a cat will do everything it can to get out of any building, and if they have kittens they will take the kittens with them. In the hours before an earthquake hits, cats get extremely agitated. They have often been seen scratching at doors to be let out, or simply hurrying outside. The Chinese always used to rely on cats to predict earthquakes and other natural disasters. It is likely that cats are more sensitive to faint tremors or changes in magnetic fields than Uprights are. So, if your cat suddenly picks up its kittens and heads for the door maybe you should follow.

Cat Fact 70

Cats have an astonishing ability to find their way home. The most likely explanation is that cats can find their way home using the earth's magnetic field. (I explored this phenomenon in my book *Bodypower* because there is some evidence that human beings used to have this skill, have lost it, but can regain it if they try.) Cats usually travel from a new home back to an old home but there are stories of cats finding their way from their old homes to their owners' new homes. For example, a cat named Tom once travelled over 2,500 miles, from Florida to California, to find his owners in their new home. (I have no idea how the owners could have abandoned such a loving, devoted and loyal cat. The journey took just over two years.

There are many other well-authenticated stories of cats which have found their way home across vast distances. Here are one or two:

- After she was sent to Nebraska a cat called Cookie travelled 550 miles back to her home in Chicago.

- A cat called Howie travelled across 1,000 miles of wilderness and desert in the Australian outback to find his owner when she moved home. Howie's adventure included crossing several rivers.

- Kuzya, a Russian cat, travelled 1,300 miles across Siberia to get back together with his Uprights. Kuzya got lost when his family was travelling on holiday. After weeks of desperate searching the desolate Uprights eventually gave up and went home. But Kuzya turned up three months later in perfect health.

Cat Fact 71

Caterwauling is the ear-splitting sound made when cats dispute territory. The sounds vary but the message is the same: 'Puss off. You're on my territory.'

Cat Fact 72

Cats have been used to carry messages – usually in their collars. In the 1890's a pair of young lovers in Holland, who were kept apart because their respective parents did not approve of the match, used to communicate entirely by tucking little love notes into the collar of a cat who moved freely between both of their homes. The story has a happy ending. The two lovers fixed an assignation, met and ran away together to live in the village of Edam. (Where the cheese comes from). That's not the happy ending. The happy ending is that they took the cat with them. Even more extraordinary (and I haven't been able to find any official documentation so I really can't vouch for this one) is the claim made by one authority that in 1879 in Liege, Belgium, 37 cats were employed to carry bundles of letters to local villages. It is said that this postal experiment was abandoned when the cats were found to be unreliable and had to be retired, presumably on half pay.

Cat Fact 73

A cat called Mickey, who earned a living as a mouser for 23 years at a British company called Shepherd and Sons Ltd, is reported to have killed more than 22,000 mice.

Cat Fact 74

In 1602 the Japanese Government gave all adult cats their freedom and prohibited the buying or selling of them. The Government even passed a law making it illegal to give cats to anyone as presents.

Cat Fact 75

When a cat is relaxing it will gradually close its eyes. If a cat closes its eyes when in your presence it is showing that it trusts you and has confidence in you. Either that or it has simply gone to sleep. Again.

Cat Fact 76

A female cat can be impregnated by several tomcats one after the other. Multiple impregnation is also known as superfecundation and one surprising consequence is that kittens in the same litter may have more than one father. This can give big problems to the Kitten Support Agency when it is trying to decide whom to contact.

Cat Fact 77

A kitten which is not handled and exposed to a wide variety of experiences and stimulations between the ages of two and seven weeks may grow up to be particularly nervous around Uprights.

Cat Fact 78

During deep sleep cats may twitch their whiskers, move their tails or flex their paws. Scientists who have studied the electrical activity in a cat's brain during sleep (which can be done without harming the cat in any way) are certain that cats dream because cats have the sort of brain activity during sleep that is associated with dreaming in Uprights. So, when Tiddles quietly growls and reaches out with a paw while apparently fast asleep on the sofa the chances are that he really is dreaming of chasing rabbits.

Cat Fact 79

Cats tend to play for longer when they have started the game than they do when an Upright has started the game.

Cat Fact 80

Independent people, loners with artistic temperaments, tend to prefer cats to dogs. Team players, who prefer a regimented, more organised life, tend to prefer dogs. Neither is right. They are just different.

Cat Fact 81

White cats are often deaf and white cats with blue eyes are more likely to be deaf than white cats with orange eyes. A white cat with one blue eye and one orange eye which is deaf in one ear will probably be deaf in the ear next to the blue eye. Got that?

Cat Fact 82

Between the 12th and 17th centuries cats were persecuted because their shining eyes convinced people that they had demonic powers. Throughout Europe cats were stoned, burnt and hurled from towers because they were feared to have black powers. This was a mistake for which the cat-killers paid a heavy price. When the Crusaders came back from the Holy Land with plague carrying Asiatic black rats hiding in their luggage there were no cats left to kill the rats. And so the rats spread throughout Europe. And so did the plague. The result: rather a lot of Uprights died.

Cat Fact 83

A new-born kitten cannot urinate or defaecate unless its mother licks the appropriate region. Unless the mother is there the kitten cannot pass waste material until it is about three weeks old.

Cat Fact 84

The world's oldest cat, who died in April 1998, was called Rexand. He was 34 years, 2 months and 4 hours old when he died. The previous holder was a female Tabby called Ma who died in 1957 aged 34 years and a day.

Cat Fact 85

When cats drink they usually lap four or five times before they swallow. Slurp, slurp, slurp, slurp swallow, slurp, slurp, slurp, slurp, swallow...

Cat Fact 86

Scottish Fold cats appear to have no ears because their ears are folded tightly along their head. The breed was first spotted in 1961 by a Scottish shepherd, though just where the cats had all been hiding up until then is something of a mystery to me.

Cat Fact 87

A cat's ears have five times as many muscles as an Upright's ears (thirty compared to six). As a result cats can rotate their ears in all sorts of interesting directions and can listen to all sorts of interesting conversations that Uprights tend to miss.

Cat Fact 88

Cats can move fluidly because they have so many muscles.

Cat Fact 89

Manx cats are reputed to have lost their tails when getting on board Noah's Ark. Two Manx cats were the last creatures to board the ark and Noah rather clumsily let the door slam shut on the cats' tails.

Cat Fact 90

When a cat swallows a mouse (or, indeed, any other small mammal) it ingests the mouse with the grain of the mouse's hair (rather than against it).

Cat Fact 91

When a cat eats a bird it will always remove the feathers first.

Cat Fact 92

A war correspondent called Labouchere claimed to have eaten cats and kittens during the siege of Paris in 1870. 'A cat is something between a rabbit and a squirrel, with a flavour of its own,' he wrote afterwards. 'It is delicious. Don't drown your kittens, eat them.'

Cat Fact 93

In early 19th century a disgusting Frenchman called Terrare of Versailles would eat whole raw cats. Half an hour after eating a cat he would regurgitate a ball of skin and fur. You wouldn't want him at a dinner party would you?

Cat Fact 94

Natives of the Trobriand Islands (part of Papua New Guinea) used to eat roasted cat stuffed with mice when they felt like a celebration.

Cat Fact 95

People who like eating cats are officially called 'ailurovores'. Unofficially they are called something else entirely less attractive.

Cat Fact 96

Cats are attracted to people who are frightened of cats because people who are nervous about cats tend to stand still and look away. Cats like this. The best way to send a cat away is to move about and look straight into its eyes. And that, ironically, is what cat lovers often do when unsuccessfully trying to attract a cat's attention.

Cat Fact 97

Cats are, traditionally, the only animals allowed in convents. The English Nuns' Rule, dated 1205, says: 'Dear Sisters, you must keep no beast other than a cat.'

Cat Fact 98

Americans spend more on cat food than baby food. Their expenditure on cat food more than doubles every decade and currently runs into several billion dollars a year.

Cat Fact 99

Cats prefer their food to be served at a temperature of 86 degrees Fahrenheit. This is the same as the body temperature of a cat. And, more crucially, it is the same as the body temperature of a mouse.

Cat Fact 100

The more food you give a cat the less it will wander. Researchers with nothing better to do have noted that the more food cats are given the smaller their territories become. Gosh, what a surprise that must have been.

Cat Fact 101

Cathaulling used to be torturing someone by getting a cat to claw them. Today cathaul simply means to question someone rather intensely. However, now that torture has come back into fashion with both the American and British Governments who knows what the future will hold.

Cat Fact 102

There is a temple in Tokyo (the temple of Go-To-Ku-Ji) which is dedicated to cats. There are painted, carved and sculptured cats there, in addition to graves of genuine cats.

Cat Fact 103

The saying 'Give the cat another goldfish' means 'Oh, let's have another biscuit (beer, whisky, doughnut, slice of cake).'

Cat Fact 104
A group of domestic cats may be known as a 'glaring', a 'clutter' or a 'clowder' of cats. A group of wild cats is called a `dout of cats' or `a destruction of cats'.

Cat Fact 105
Cats, like people are either right or left handed or, to be more precise, either right or left pawed. But the proportions aren't the same. Roughly half of all cats favour their right paw and half favour their left.

Cat Fact 106
The phrase 'having kittens', used to express anxiety and the associated abdominal pains (caused either by irritable bowel syndrome or gastritis) originated in the Middle Ages when it was believed that pregnant women who were in great pain had kittens clawing at their wombs. In 1654 a Scottish woman went to court to seek an abortion because, she said, she had kittens in her womb.

Cat Fact 107
A cat's heart normally beats at around 240 beats a minute. That is approximately four times the rate of a normal, healthy human heart.

Cat Fact 108
Cats have amazing hearing and are particularly good at identifying high pitched sounds. A cat can accurately distinguish between a rustling and a scratching at some distance and cats can even distinguish mice from shrews by the noise they make moving through undergrowth.

Cat Fact 109
Cats use their hearing more than their sight when they are out hunting. Cats can hear much better than dogs. Uprights can distinguish sounds up to 20,000 cycles per second. Dogs can manage up to 40,000 cycles per second. But cats can distinguish sounds up to 100,000 cycles per second. This proves conclusively and scientifically that cats are two and a half times better than dogs.

Cat Fact 110

Cats are very good at identifying the direction from which a sound emanates. At sixty feet a cat can distinguish between two sounds that are just eighteen inches apart. And cats can easily differentiate between two sounds that differ by a halftone.

Cat Fact 111

Look carefully at the word 'homeowner' and you'll see that there is a meow in the middle of it.

Cat Fact 112

A cat's hiss does not mean that the cat will start fighting. Cats practice Aikido – preferring not to attack first but to wait for the other animal to attack. This can result in two aggressive cats circling and hissing and snarling and glowering and generally doing a great deal of threatening before there is any action. Two cats can get into a staring match that will last for up to half an hour. At the end of the staring match there is a chance that the two cats will merely retreat, to avoid an actual fight. Cats often retreat (slowly) to avoid actually having to get involved in an unseemly brawl. It isn't the injuries they are frightened of, but the prospect of looking unkempt afterwards.

Cat Fact 113

A cat's pupils dilate when it is hungry and finds food. A cat's pupils can enlarge at a phenomenally fast rate and can dilate to five times their previous size in less than one second.

Cat Fact 114

Scientists claim that wild cats (aka feral cats) may spend as much as twelve out of every 24 hours hunting for food. Since scientists also claim that cats spend two thirds of their lives sleeping this means that wild cats must spend four hours a day hunting while they are asleep. Don't blame me for this contradiction. I just write the books.

Cat Fact 115

The Japanese used to draw pictures of cats on their doors in the belief that this would keep mice away. Japanese house owners also used to decorate their homes with cats made of wood, bronze and porcelain for the same reason.

Cat Fact 116

Cats are independent and hunt alone, rather than in packs. Dogs are pack animals who hunt in a group. Dogs regard Uprights as pack-leaders because they provide food and leadership. Cats, not being accustomed to working with others do not recognise leadership and will, at best, regard a relationship with an Upright as a relationship between equals. A cat will love you and cherish you and enjoy your company but it will not fetch your slippers, make your tea or run your bath.

Cat Fact 117

The Kilkenny Cats are legendary Irish cats who are reputed to have fought so hard that in the end only their tails remained. I suspect that this myth may not be entirely reliable.

Cat Fact 118

Cats sometimes get diarrhoea if they drink cows' milk because they are short of lactase, the enzyme used to digest lactose. Cows' milk is an excellent food for calves but not a terribly suitable or useful food for other creatures such as Uprights or cats.

Cat Fact 119

During the French Revolution of 1789, the cat was used as a symbol of liberty. The Swiss have for many centuries regarded the cat as a symbol of freedom. And Libertas, the Roman goddess of liberty, had a cat lying by her feet.

Cat Fact 120

Cats are almost alone among animals in never having been tried in the

English criminal courts. Pigs, bulls and dogs have all been tried for criminal offences – but never cats.

Cat Fact 121

The Roman Catholic Church has excommunicated all sorts of animals. But it has never excommunicated a cat.

Cat Fact 122

Cats don't like using a litter tray which is too close to their food. And can you blame them? Have you ever smelt the contents of a cat litter tray?

Cat Fact 123

A cat's paw is the name sailors give to a light breeze that just ruffles the surface of the water.

Cat Fact 124

A cat's purr is supposed to be medical slang for the sound which doctors hear with a stethoscope when listening to a faulty mitral valve in the heart. (However, I've never heard doctors use this term which seems to me to be too contrived and twee for medical purposes. Doctors tend to use rougher images. For example anaesthetists are known in the trade as 'gasmen' or 'gassers' and thoracic surgeons are known as 'chest cutters'.)

Cat Fact 125

A cat's tail is said to be meteorological slang for a cirrus cloud which looks like a cat's tail. Small white fluffy clouds which race across the sky are sometimes known as kittens.

Cat Fact 126

Schoolboys of an older generation will know that a cat's eye aggie is an agate marble. Modern schoolboys don't play marbles unless it is available as a computer game.

Cat Fact 127

A catcall was originally a squeaky whistle which members of the audience used in British music halls when they weren't entirely happy with the quality of a performance. The word has been used for this purpose since at least 1659. Today the word 'catcall' describes any derisory sound made by an unhappy audience member.

Cat Fact 128

A cathouse is a brothel. The Americans like to think that they invented this usage of the word. However, the word 'cat' has been slang for a prostitute since the 15th century so it's fairly safe to assume it originated in England and most probably in London. The two became associated because of the way that city Queens who are in heat will attract tomcats (and then mate with them indiscriminately).

Cat Fact 129

Catgut, used to make surgical sutures and strings for tennis racquets and musical instruments has nothing whatsoever to do with cats. It is made from the intestines of sheep and horses. The word catgut is a bastardisation of the word kitgut and the 'kit' part of this word means 'small fiddle'.

Cat Fact 130

The word 'catrigged' means badly creased linen.

Cat Fact 131

The phrase 'fighting like cats and dogs' is misleading. It is a myth that cats and dogs are natural enemies. A cat and a dog who share the same home will often get on together better than two cats or two dogs. But the myth is now far too well-ingrained to be eradicated.

Cat Fact 132

A chatiere is a small opening in a door – made so that a cat can get in and out easily. The French, who adore cats, used to cut these holes in their doors as far back as the 16th century. (It took an Englishman, Sir

Isaac Newton, to take time off from rubbing his head, picking up apples and discovering gravity to invent the cat flap so that cats could get in and out without subjecting the humans inside to a constant draught.)

Cat Fact 133

Cats which go up trees usually come down again by themselves. The rule of thumb is that if a cat does not come down within 48 hours then you should call the Fire Brigade. Before doing this, however, try opening a can of tuna, putting it on the ground underneath the tree, leaving the area and waiting.

Cat Fact 134

Since the late 1920's the British Civil Service has kept details of the cats employed on Government service. On the 3rd June 1929, an official request was made for an allowance of one penny per day for a mouser named Peter who was employed at the Home Office. Peter was succeeded by a series of male cats with the same name until in 1964 a pedigree Manx female was appointed to a non-industrial grade and given the name Peta. Her aristocratic temperament meant that she neglected her duties and became 'inordinately fat'. Staff were instructed not to give her titbits. She kept her job until 1976 when she retired to live in the country and fertilise roses.

Cat Fact 135

Famous circus entrepreneur P. T. Barnum once let it be known that he was looking for a cherry coloured cat to add to his circus. A man who lived in Vermont wrote to say that he had a cherry coloured cat whom he would sell. Barnum paid for the cat and sent extra money to have it shipped to him. When the great circus man opened the crate he found that it contained a fairly ordinary looking black cat who had a ribbon around its neck. Tied to the ribbon was a message which said: 'Up in Vermont, the cherries are black.'

Cat Fact 136

Cats wash a great deal in order to get rid of any odours which might scare off their prey. (They also lick themselves to keep cool, because they like it and because they pick up vitamin D excreted by their own hair follicles.)

Cat Fact 137

Domestic cats bury their excrement in order to prevent their prey knowing that they are around as much as they do it to protect themselves from predators. Wild cats, particularly aggressive ones, are likely to leave their excrement uncovered, and often in particularly conspicuous places, to taunt and threaten any other animals which might pass by.

Cat Fact 138

In addition to the Frenchman Pierre-Auguste Renoir (see Cat Fact 9), famous artists who have painted cats include: the Italian Leonardo da Vinci, the Dutchman Harmenszoon van Rijn Rembrandt, the Spaniards Francisco de Goya and Pablo Picasso, the Frenchmen, Marc Chagall and Eugene Delacroix, the German Albrecht Durer and the Swiss Paul Klee.

Leonardo da Vinci, Italian painter, musician, sculptor, engineer, architect, inventor, scientist, thinker and all round genius and signature artist for the Italian Renaissance is famous among cat lovers for having said that 'the smallest feline is a masterpiece'. There are some predictably marvellous cat drawings of his in a gallery in Florence. The drawings

A cathouse is a brothel.

include cats fighting and licking their bottoms. It is rumoured among cat lovers that da Vinci's original draft for his painting of the Madonna included a cat in the Madonna's arms. (The absence of the cat might explain why the model looks rather miffed.)

Rembrandt's work includes The Virgin and Child with Cat. Rembrandt used cats to help him create domestic scenes.

Pablo Picasso produced a picture called *Cat and Bird*. The cat is attacking the bird and is said to be symbolic of the cruelty of General Franco's fascist regime in Spain.

Russian born French painter Marc Chagall drew cats with human faces and drew humans with cat faces. Famous works by Chagall include: *The Cat Transformed Into A Woman.*

Paintings by Paul Klee, the Swiss artist, include one called *Cat and Bird* in which a bird is perched on the forehead of a wide eyed, watchful cat.

Cat Fact 139
Black cats are associated with good luck in Britain but with bad luck in America and continental Europe.

Cat Fact 140
The white mark running from a cat's forehead to its nose is called a blaze.

Cat Fact 141
The white markings on the backs of the rear legs of cats are called laces.

Cat Fact 142
The white markings around a cat's feet are called socks, gloves or mittens.

Cat Fact 143
A white or coloured patch under a cat's neck is called a locket.

Cat Fact 144

Between 1570 and 1970 approximately 3,200 cat books were published.

Cat Fact 145

The two most popular cat stories are *Dick Whittington* and *Puss in Boots*.

Cat Fact 146

In California (which really ought to be renamed Catifornia) cats seeking luxuries can take advantage of:

- cat psychiatrists
- a pussycat dating service
- a cat department store
- a cat resort
- a feline rest home
- a rent–a–cat agency
- cat psychics
- feline acting coaches
- an annual meowing contest

Cat Fact 147

Blunt speaking Britons claim that they call a spade a spade. Blunt speaking French folk say they call a cat a cat (well, actually, they call a chat a chat).

Cat Fact 148

Cats need taurine, an amino acid which they cannot manufacture from non-animal sources, they need vitamins which are only found in animal foods and they need animal fats in order to manufacture essential fatty acids. So, I'm afraid it isn't possible for a cat to survive and stay healthy on a purely vegetarian diet.

Cat Fact 149

The phrase 'playing cat and mouse' goes back centuries but was made popular when the British Parliament passed *The Prisoners (Temporary Discharge for Ill-health) Act of 1913*. The act was passed to stop suffragettes martyring themselves by going on hunger strike. Prisoners could be released from prison while fasting and then rearrested when they started eating again. This was dubbed the *Cat and Mouse Act*.

Cat Fact 150

A 'cat whipper' is a lazy worker. The phrase is synonymous with 'clock watcher' and 'bench warmer'.

Cat Fact 151

A 'cat with two legs' is a phrase used when the cat has been falsely blamed. So, when an ornament has been broken and a child blames the cat his mother, suspecting that the boy was the true culprit, might say: 'Yes, a cat with two legs.'

Cat Fact 152

The phrase 'a cat in hell's chance' is actually an abbreviation of the expression 'no more chance than a cat in hell without claws'. It suggests that someone who is insufficiently well armed (against whatever enemy they might face) will be helpless.

Cat Fact 153

The existence of Batman and Catwoman are well known. It is less well known that there has been a character called Cat-Man. Various artists drew Cat-Man in American comics running through the 1930's and 1940's. The best known series was the one drawn by Charles Quinlan in the early 1940's. Cat-Man's real name (in the comic) was David Merrywether. Mr Merrywether was the sole survivor of a group of Americans who had been attacked by Burmese bandits. He was cared for by a variety of wild animals and eventually went to America to fight crime (presumably because there was more of it there than anywhere else). He wore an orange tunic with a C on the chest and had a cape with a hood. He was killed more often than most superheroes would have found comfortable but had nine lives so this was not too much of a problem. He had a sidekick called The Kitten.

Cat Fact 154

A cat's breakfast (like a dog's breakfast) is anything that is a mess or confused.

Cat Fact 155

Whether they are right or left pawed, cats usually pounce with both paws if they are catching insects or birds. When catching mice and other small rodents, however, they usually strike with their dominant paw only and then bite the unfortunate creature on the neck. If the bite is ineffective, perhaps because the prey is too large, the cat will hold on with its teeth and then bash at its victim with its paws.

Cat Fact 156

Cats will often learn things which appear to undiscerning Uprights to be tricks. Clever Uprights who really do understand cats will, of course, realise that the cat has merely learned to do something which it finds to its advantage. So, for example, cats have learned to open doors (by leaping up and catching the handle), press doorbells (by leaping up and bashing the bell with a paw), use flushing toilets (by squatting over the bowel and then pressing the flush lever) and turn on lights (by pressing the required switch). My dear friend, the much lamented late Alice, learned to switch on my electric typewriter (back in the days when such things were fashionable) because she liked the humming, purring sound it made and because she knew that when it had been switched on for a while it grew quite warm. In all these instances cats learned how to do something not, as a dog will, because they want to impress an Upright, but because there was some clear advantage to them in learning how to do it.

Cat Fact 157

A four-month-old kitten owned by Josephine Aufdenblatten of Geneva, Switzerland, climbed to the top of the Matterhorn, nearly 15,000 feet high, in 1950.

Cat Fact 158

In the late 1940's a black female cat called Mincha got stuck up a 40 foot tree in Buenos Aires, Argentina. Mincha is reported to have made the tree her home for the next six years. During this time male cats must have got up and down the tree successfully because Mincha managed to give birth to three litters of kittens without coming down. She was fed by locals who sent up meals via long poles but who, presumably, did not spend too much time standing underneath the tree.

Cat Fact 159

During the First World War the British employed around 500,000 cats as official ratters and mousers in the trenches. The cats were also expected to warn troops if clouds of poison gas were coming.

Cat Fact 160

It is a pleasant and well-sustained myth that a cat uses its whiskers to help maintain its balance. Whiskers play very little part in enabling a cat to walk along narrow ledges. Whiskers aren't entirely ornamental, however. A cat does use its whiskers to feel its way through gaps.

Cat Fact 161

A black and white cat named Tom got lost in the hold of a British Airways plane for two months. During that time he travelled more than 500,000 miles.

Cat Fact 162

A cat called Hamlet escaped from his cage on a flight from Toronto, Canada and travelled 600,000 miles before he was caught and rescued 7 months later.

Cat Fact 163

A cat called Princess Truman Tai-Tai travelled over 1,500,000 miles (in 16 years) while employed by the British ship Sagamire as a mouser and ratter.

Cat Fact 164

In 1868, the Cat System was introduced in London. Three cats were employed as mousers in public buildings on a pretty decent salary (for the time) of two shillings a week.

Cat Fact 165

The first pair of breeding Siamese cats arrived in England in 1884.

Cat Fact 166

Lilies and lily pollen are lethal to cats. Eating just one lily leaf can kill a cat.

Cat Fact 167

A cat called Zizou was adopted by a mountaineering club at Mont Blanc on the borders of France, Italy and Switzerland because she often followed mountaineers to the top of the 15,771 foot peak.

Cat Fact 168

In 1928, a cat was found in a hut belonging to a mountaineering club 9,000 feet above sea level in the Swiss Alps. No one knew how or why the cat had got there but it was adopted as the hut's official caretaker and would often follow climbers to over 12,000 feet.

Cat Fact 169

A seven-year-old Burmese cat called Lilac is Britain's best known cat burglar. He gets into strange homes through the cat-flap and steals anything he can carry away. Over the years he has stolen six teddy bears, three cuddly rabbits, a polo-neck sweater, two cushions, three feather dusters and an assortment of other toys. He was reported to be seeing a cat psychologist.

Cat Fact 170

Here's a list of how to say 'to purr' in a variety of different languages (my favourite is the Korean):

- Danish: spindle

- Dutch: snorren
- English: to purr
- Finnish: kehrata
- French: ronronner
- German: schnurren
- Greek: niaourizee
- Hawaiian: nonolo
- Hebrew: yeemyom
- Hindi: billi ney awaaz
- Hungarian: dorombol
- Italian: fare le fusa
- Japanese: gorogoro
- Korean: grr grrr
- Norwegian: myrreng
- Polish: mruczec
- Portugese: ronronar
- Romania: face ate
- Spain: ronronear
- Turkish: mirlar
- Welsh: grwnan

Cat Fact 171

When his Upright died in 1963, a cat called Brownie in California inherited £217,000. But this was nothing. A man called Ben Rea left his cat Blackie a far more spectacular £14 million. How long would it take to spend that lot on fresh salmon and cat litter?

Cat Fact 172

Polydactyly (having an extra digit on each paw, or in the case of Uprights, hand or, foot) is most commonly found in cats wandering around sea ports. This is simply because sailors have always preferred such cats as mousers.

Cat Fact 173

A cat called Jake, who lives in Ontario, Canada, has 7 toes on each paw – 28 toes in all. Each toe has its own complete bone structure, claw and pad. Second place in the 'having-a-lot-of-toes competition' is held by a tabby cat called Mickey who lived in New York, USA, and had 27 toes.

Cat Fact 174

American President George W. Bush had a cat called India sent away from the White House because of his tendency to scratch the furniture.

Cat Fact 175

It was the British who spread cats (and cat loving) around the world. It is for this reason that throughout the world, particularly in former British colonies, a great many tabby cats can be found. The blotched or mixed tabby is sometimes known as the British Imperial cat.

Cat Fact 176

Domenico Balestrieri asked 80 eminent friends to write mourning poems in Italian, Arabic, French, Latin and Greek for his deceased tabby. The collection, entitled *Tears on the Death of a Cat,* was published in Milan in 1741.

Cat Fact 177

When the great American writer Mark Twain (aka Samuel Clemens) was about to enter a room, two kittens suddenly appeared. Twain opened the door, bowed to the kittens and said: 'Walk in, gentlemen. I always give precedence to royalty.'

Cat Fact 178

Controversial 19th century French poet Charles Baudelaire, who wrote three poems to cats, would never greet the human inhabitants of a home which he was visiting until he had thoroughly caressed all the available cats.

Cat Fact 179

The Italian painter Faustino Bocchi frequently included cats in his paintings. One of Bocchi's paintings shows a cat being given a full spa treatment by a team of devoted dwarves who are brushing its tail and grooming its fur.

Cat Fact 180

When the pianist Ignace Paderewski first appeared in concert as a soloist in London the theatre's resident cat jumped into his lap as he was playing his first piece. The audience was delighted. The pianist, to his eternal credit, let the cat stay on his lap. (There might have been some conflict had the cat chosen instead to settle on the keyboard.)

Cat Fact 181

The artist John Spencer Churchill had a long-haired tabby called Princess Sophie Louise of Sweden. When the Princess Sophie first arrived in his household Churchill elevated his black cat Lady Arabella a rank or two and made her the Duchess of Catalunya and Countess of Barcelona.

Cat Fact 182

Robert Southey (the English poet) gradually elevated his cat Lord Nelson to Baron, then Viscount and finally Earl for services performed against rats.

Cat Fact 183

Thriller writer Raymond Chandler described his black Persian cat Taki as his secretary because she insisted on sitting on his manuscripts when he was working on them. (As far as I am aware there is no record of whether or not he claimed her services as a tax deductible expense.)

Cat Fact 184

Charles I, the more than ever so slightly stupid King of England, Scotland and Ireland whose potty and arrogant behaviour led England into a long and bloody civil war, kept a black cat who he believed brought him luck. (Heaven knows what would have happened without the cat). He was so afraid that the animal would disappear or be stolen that he had it guarded night and day. It seems that his fears were well founded. On the day after the cat died Charles was arrested and subsequently beheaded in Whitehall.

Cat Fact 185

Koko, a female gorilla, had a Manx kitten which she named Lips-Lipstick. 'My cat good', said Koko one day, though she used sign language to pass this observation on to her keepers.

Cat Fact 186

The oldest cat on record to give birth was a queen who, in 1987, gave birth to two healthy kittens. The cat was 30 at the time. (This is roughly equivalent to a woman of 150 having babies.)

Cat Fact 187

In Victorian households it was not unusual for little girls to be told to model themselves on cats. Girls were told that in order to grow up into ladies they should try to imitate the cat's poise, grace, cleanliness and maternal skills.

Cat Fact 188

When the Earl of Southampton was imprisoned for treason and kept in the Tower of London, his faithful cat Trixie kept him company. During the Earl's two years in prison Trixie regularly made her way across London and got into and out of his cell via the chimney. The Earl was so impressed with the cat's loyalty that when he eventually got out he commissioned a portrait of himself and Trixie pictured together in his cell. (Big deal. I bet Trixie would have preferred a nice plump rabbit.)

Cat Fact 189

When Tigger's Uprights moved to a new home three miles away they took their cat with them. But Tigger wasn't so eager to move. In just two years the six-year-old cat made 76 visits to his previous home. Tigger had only three legs, having lost one leg in a road accident when he was a kitten.

Cat Fact 190

The first recorded cat hotel was opened in Philadelphia, Pennsylvania, USA and had accommodation for over 100 cats in individual rooms furnished with soft rugs. Meals were served from plates at a dining table and the hotel had a personal hairdresser.

Cat Fact 191

A British woman received an official warning from the Post Office that they would no longer deliver mail to her address unless she kept her cat, Snoopy under control. Snoopy, allegedly a normally placid cat, took a dislike to the postman and carried out several unprovoked attacks on him. She ambushed him from behind a fir tree, scratched his hand as he pushed mail through the letter box and stalked him across the lawn. It is believed that the cat objected to the way the mail tended to block up her cat flap.

Cat Fact 192

The French physician, astrologer and author Michel de Notre Dame, who is better remembered as Nostradamus, had a cat called Grimalkin. (Grimalkin is an archaic English word meaning cat. It is derived from two words 'grey' and 'malkin'. Malkin is a pet version of the name Matilda. So you could say, if you really wanted to, that Nostradamus had a cat called Grey Matilda. Not a lot of people know that, as they say.)

Cat Fact 193

When USA President Calvin Coolidge's cat Tiger disappeared the President (who didn't say much and was known as the silent President) went on the radio and broadcast an appeal for help in finding his beloved cat. This was a brave move for a President who didn't like saying much.

Cat Fact 194

The Egyptians, who loved and revered cats, rather liked the fact that cats are independent creatures. They felt that this showed that when cats lived with them it was because they chose to do so rather than because they needed to.

Cat Fact 195

When his much loved white cat died, Charles Sonnini de Manoncourt wrote: 'Unfortunately for mankind, the life of the wicked is long. Those audacious, criminal and execrable men, whose names my pen should trace, were it not reserved to Heaven to signalise against them its justice, are yet alive; while my beautiful and interesting companion is no more. After several days of suffering, during which I never left her, her eyes, constantly fixed on me, closed never again to open – my tears flowed – they now flow. Feeling minds will pardon this digression, the result of grief and gratitude. Those whose souls are rendered callous by egotism and insensibility, give me no disquiet; it is not for them I write.'

Cat Fact 196

The word 'Mao' is Chinese for cat.

Cat Fact 197

The word used to describe the noise a cat makes has more accepted spelling variations than any other common four letter English word. All of them sound remarkably like the noise a cat makes. Here are the main variations

- miaou
- maiow
- meaow
- meaw
- meeow
- mew
- miaou
- miaouw

- miaow
- miau
- miauw
- miaw
- mieaou (the shortest word in the English language containing all five vowels)
- miow
- miowe

Cat Fact 198

Cats like being stroked because being stroked reminds them of their mother's affection. Mother cats lick their kittens a lot when they are small, and when an Upright strokes a cat the cat is reminded of the good feeling it had when it was being licked by its mother.

Cat Fact 199

When a cat waves its tail it is showing conflict. If a cat is confused its tail will wave as it struggles to decide what to do. So, for example, if a cat is standing in the doorway because it wants to go outside, but it notices that it is starting to rain, it will stand and wave its tail about as it tries to come to a decision.

Cat Fact 200

Most cats' eyes are greenish yellowish goldish.

Cat Fact 201

Cats are long-sighted and objects close to them seem rather fuzzy. They cannot see things directly underneath them. Their peripheral vision is, however, very good.

Cat Fact 202

In proportion to the size of their bodies, cats have the largest eyes of any mammal.

Cat Fact 203

It is not true that cats are colour blind. Recent research has shown that cats can see separate colours.

Cat Fact 204

Cats' curiosity can get them into lots of trouble. Cats have been locked in suitcases and in tradesmen's delivery vehicles. Cats love jumping up onto shelves where there is room for a vase or a cat but not both.

Cats love jumping up onto shelves where there
is room for a vase or a cat but not both

Cat Fact 205

Cats can see six times better than Uprights in the dark (or, to put it another way, they need only a sixth of the amount of light to see just as well).

Cat Fact 206

Cats like to develop habits for eating. They like to be fed at the same time and in the same place – preferably a quiet spot where they are not likely to be watched, interrupted or threatened.

Cat Fact 207

Raw and undercooked meat, and raw eggs, are dangerous for cats.

Cat Fact 208

A cat living in the wild would, all things being equal, eat 10 mice a day. This is perhaps why cats prefer regular small (mouse-sized) meals.

Cat Fact 209

Cats need more protein than dogs and so dog food isn't suitable for cats. Even if they would eat it. Which they won't.

Cat Fact 210

Cats don't normally eat fish. Most wild cats won't bother to catch fish even when the fish are readily available and catchable. There is, however, a breed of cat in India which hunts for fish on a regular basis.

Cat Fact 211

There are three possible explanations for the phrase 'it is raining cats and dogs'.

First, it may be taken from the phrase 'it is raining catadoupes'. The word catadoupe is an ancient word for waterfall and sounds vaguely similar to 'cats and dogs'.

Second, when it rained a lot in the 17th century the streets and gutters may well have been awash with dead dogs and cats.

Third, Norse mythology associates both dogs and cats with storms.

Cat Fact 212

Cats sometimes want to go out and then come straight back in again because they like to make brief surveys of their territory before settling down. When they get outside they probably won't want to stay out unless something interesting is going on.

Cat Fact 213
All kittens have blue eyes when they are born.

Cat Fact 214
Cats' eyes appear to glow in the dark because the cat's eye uses a reflector to maximise the amount of light available. Using the name 'cats' eyes' to describe reflectors used on roads is very apt.

Cat Fact 215
Like Uprights, cats' pupils contract and enlarge with the amount of light available. But whereas our pupils stay round, a cat's pupils will become vertical slits when the light is bright.

Cat Fact 216
Siamese cats appear to have red eyes in the dark. This is because the reflective area in their retinas lacks pigment. The red colour is actually the blood vessels there.

Cat Fact 217
Some garden plants may prove poisonous to cats. A large area of freshly dug soft earth, free of weeds and plants of all kinds, is the sort of garden cats prefer.

Cat Fact 218
When cats are asleep they are alert to stimuli of all kinds and will waken quickly.

Cat Fact 219
New born kittens sleep 90% of the time. Adult cats sleep two thirds of the time. A 10-year-old cat will have spent more than six years sleeping.

Cat Fact 220

Cats who are told off will turn their backs on their Uprights and refuse to look at them. This is because the Upright has tried to dominate the cat. The cat is turning its back on the Upright to stop this absurd piece of Upright impertinence.

Cat Fact 221

One female cat and her offspring, left to their own devices and allowed to breed at will (and with an abundant supply of tomcats) would, in seven years, produce 400,000 descendants.

Cat Fact 222

Cats can meow, hiss, purr, growl, mew, caterwaul and use many gestures (fur raising, facial expressions, posture) to get across what they feel. One expert, Mildred Moelk, claimed in 1944 that cats produce 16 different meaningful sounds – a mixture of vowels, consonants and diphthongs. Cats can change the meaning of their meow by altering tone, pitch, rhythm, pronunciation and volume.

Cat Fact 223

The English poet Chaucer recommended that cats should be given plenty of milk, lots of tender meat and a cushion of silk to sleep on.

Cat Fact 224

People who say they are allergic to cats are usually allergic to the dander (or dead skin flakes) in the cat's fur. Bathing the cat regularly with the most expensive cat shampoo available will probably stop the problem though it will, of course, create another problem – as anyone who has ever tried to shampoo a cat will confirm.

Cat Fact 225

Cats like warm climates. They can tolerate a skin temperature of 126 degrees Fahrenheit before they start to complain of the heat. This is far more than most Uprights can possibly put up with.

Cat Fact 226

Scientists in America have discovered that the frequency at which a cat purrs helps its bones and organs to mend and stimulates the skeletal system, preventing bones from weakening.

Cat Fact 227

According to one group of psychologists people who keep dogs are looking for love. They desperately need to be loved and so they choose to share their lives with dogs – which offer love unconditionally. Cat lovers, on the other hand, have lots of love to give and keep cats so that they have an animal to love.

Cat Fact 228

The Americans are famous for many things, not least their vast repertoire of daft laws. Britain has some pretty potty laws but at least we have the excuse that most of our really hare-brained ones date back to the Middle Ages. American legislators have no such excuse. Here are some dotty American laws which deal with cats:

1. Cats who live in Montana are legally obliged to wear three bells around their necks. The bells are there to provide a warning to birds.

2. In Natchez, Mississippi it is illegal for cats to drink beer. I have no idea what happens to cats who ignore this law.

3. Cats who live in Dallas, Texas, must wear a headlight if they go out onto the streets after dark.

4. In Idaho it is illegal for a cat to interfere in a fight between two dogs.

5. In Louisiana cats are forbidden by law from chasing ducks in city streets.

Cat Fact 229

Thomasina (the beautiful mackerel tabby cat who 'co-starred' in *Alice's Diary* and *Alice's Adventures*) was the only cat to have had an obituary in a national newspaper. The following is part of a piece which appeared in my column in the *Sunday People* on 9th April 2000:

'My very dear friend Thomasina died recently. I miss her terribly.

She lived with me for seventeen years and she never failed to comfort me when I felt low and to sustain me when I felt despair. She was always there when I felt lonely and she was, in every conceivable respect, a true and loyal friend. She shared my bed at night and during the daytime we spent many an hour playing together. In the summer we sat side by side in the garden or went on long walks together. If I had been out of the house she always met me at the door.

She was one of the most perceptive beings I have ever known and she had remarkably acute instincts. If things were going badly or if I was upset about something she would always climb onto my lap or my shoulder so that she could comfort me.

'Are you going to get another cat?' asked an acquaintance who had heard that Thomasina had died.

How can you replace a friend?

It's like saying: 'Are you going to get another mother, father, son, daughter, brother, sister, wife or husband?'

Pets make tremendous companions and can provide genuine companionship for the lonely, the elderly and the shy. There is ample evidence to show that having a cat can help produce a genuine improvement in a human 'owner's' physical and mental health.

Few things are more relaxing than stroking a cat.

There is no doubt that we benefit from their company but we can also learn a great deal from the animals we live with. Sit and watch any animal at play, or hunting, and you will learn a great deal.

What a tragedy it is, therefore, that our so-called civilised society still treats the animals with whom we share this planet with such ill-disguised contempt.

WHISTLER'S CAT | THE LAUGHING TABBY | THE LUNCH ON THE GRASS

"I know what I like."

Chapter Five

How Intelligent Is Your Cat?

This questionnaire is designed for you to complete on your cat's behalf. By the time you have completed the questionnaire, and worked out the results, you will know just how bright your cat really is. Is your cat a genius, or just very clever?

Note: I have used the phrase 'your cat' here not to denote ownership of the cat by the Upright but, rather, the other way round. Replace the word 'he' with 'she' as and when appropriate.

1. When you are preparing your cat's next meal does your cat arrive:
a)   when he hears or sees you carrying the food to put it down in the usual place
b)   when he hears the sound of the can opener or the box being opened
c)   when he hears food being put into a dish
d)   when you call him
e)   just before you call him
f)   just before you think about calling him

2. Where is your cat's favourite hiding place?
a)   under the table
b)   behind a chair
c)   in a cupboard
d)   in a box
e)   you've never found it

f)   you're never found it and are pretty confident that you never will

3. If your cat wants to wake you up does he:
a)   knock something over and make a noise
b)   sit on your chest or head
c)   miaow loudly
d)   simply wander into your dream with the result that you wake up (not knowing quite why) to find your cat sitting waiting patiently beside your bed

4. If you put your cat in front of a mirror does he:
a)   take no notice
b)   attempt to touch the reflection
c)   look at himself, admire himself and purr loudly
d)   look behind the mirror to see if there is another cat there
e)   look at you rather pityingly (as though to say 'you are shallow aren't you?') and then, when he thinks you aren't looking, lick down a couple of hairs which have somehow moved out of place

5. If you put your cat inside an escape-proof carrying cage does he/she:
a)   cry and scratch ineffectively
b)   just sit there
c)   try unsuccessfully to unfasten the catch
d)   escape within seconds

6. You have just prepared a few expensive delicacies for an important supper party. Where do you put them so that there is a half way decent chance that your cat will not be able to find them:
a)   on top of the highest cupboard in the kitchen
b)   inside the fridge
c)   inside a neighbour's fridge
d)   inside the vault at your bank

7. You buy a cheaper than usual brand of cat food but before serving it you remove it from its container and place it in an empty tin which had previously

contained the more expensive cat food which your cat usually eats. *The cheap cat food looks and smells like the 'good stuff' and it now comes out of a genuine 'good stuff' tin. What do you think are the chances of your cat being taken in by this ploy, accepting the cheap food and happily consuming it?*

a) excellent

b) quite good

c) politicians will start telling the truth before your cat will fall for such a cheap trick

8. Next door's ferocious, yappy dog gets into your garden and sits outside the French windows. The windows are locked and the dog cannot get in. But the dog can see – and be seen. Does your cat:

a) run upstairs and hide

b) cower behind the sofa

c) sit right in front of the window having a wash with the result that the frustrated dog is driven to insanity

9. Does your cat ever show signs of guilt over taking a nap at 10.30 am on a weekday morning?

a) no

b) yes

10. Unpleasant relatives are coming to tea and are likely to stay for several hours. Does your cat:

a) hang around and put up with inane comments and the unwanted attention of a psychopathic six-year-old

b) disappear thirty minutes before the visitors arrive and reappear again thirty minutes after they have disappeared

11. You want to lock your cat in a room so that you can give it a pill. The room is airtight and watertight. All exits are sealed. How long will it take your cat to escape and disappear:

a) five minutes

b) three minutes

c) one minute

12. The vet is coming. His visit has been kept secret. You have not used the word 'vet' to anyone – and especially not on the telephone. When does the cat disappear:
a)   five minutes before the vet arrives
b)   ten minutes before the vet arrives
c)   fifteen minutes before the vet arrives
d)   he doesn't disappear, but sits quietly and waits for the vet to arrive

Now check your score:
    1. a) 1 b) 1 c) 1 d) 1 e) 4 f) 6
    2. a) 1 b) 1 c) 1 d) 1 e) 4 f) 6
    3. a) 1 b) 1 c) 1 d) 3
    4. a) 1 b) 1 c) 1 d) 3
    5. a) 1 b) 1 c) 2 d) 4
    6. a) 1 b) 1 c) 3 d) 5
    7. a) 1 b) 2 c) 4
    8. a) 1 b) 1 c) 3
    9. a) 2 b) 1
    10. a) 1 b) 3
    11. a) 1 b) 2 c) 3
    12. a) 3 b) 3 c) 3 d) 1

What do your results mean?
If your cat scored 15 or less then (and I'm afraid there is no kind way to break this to you) your cat's main claims to fame are likely to be physical rather than mental. Your cat is not likely to find fame listed in the Guinness Book of Records as the only cat to be a registered Grand Master at chess. Having said that your cat is still far brighter than all dogs, politicians and estate agents.

If your cat scored 16 to 25 then things are looking brighter. You have a bright cat in your home. Your cat is without doubt more intelligent than anyone working in the media.

If your cat scored 26 or over then you are living with a furry genius. Your cat is someone you should be proud to call a friend and mentor. If he or she ever looks for a pen pal then I would suggest you look for someone of the sort of calibre of Albert Einstein.

Chapter Six

How To Give Pills To Cats
(The Guaranteed Method)

Giving pills to cats is 99% preparation, 44% perspiration, 37% hope and 82% desperation. The fact that anyone who has ever tried it once even thinks of trying it again is both a triumph of hope over experience and evidence that the love of the Upright for the cat does not acknowledge normal boundaries. It is also a sign that most of us tend to block out particularly painful memories. Giving pills to cats is one of the few human activities which genuinely requires the expenditure of blood, sweat and tears.

There are some people who claim that you can give pills to cats by hiding the pills in food. This, as anyone who has ever tried it will confirm, is laughable nonsense. When I first tried to do this I was young enough and naive enough to think that just pushing a pill in among some rabbity chunks would do. When that didn't work (the cat who was the target of this planned deceit just ate around the pill) I tried inserting the pill inside a sardine. Naturally, the cat simply ignored the sardine which had the pill inside it and ate all the other sardines. When I tried putting just one (pill enriched) sardine on the plate the cat ate the bits of sardine around the pill and left the rest. On the one occasion when the cat I was trying to medicate actually chewed a pill by mistake he spat it out immediately.

Crushing a pill and trying to hide the resulting powder in food has also always been a failure. The cats involved always simply refuse to eat any of the contaminated food. When I once tried this with my dear cat Alice she looked at me, shook her head sadly, stalked off and caught a mouse.

After many years of attempting to give pills to cats I eventually devised a system that works.

Hearing of my skills in this specialist area of cat husbandry several friends subsequently asked for copies of my aide mémoire. Their gratitude has encouraged me to reproduce here advice which was originally intended only for personal use, in the hope that others might find it useful in their hour of need.

How to give a cat a pill in lots of easy steps

1. When the vet recommends that you give pills to your cat your first step should be to cancel all your appointments for the duration of the treatment. Giving a cat a pill is a full-time occupation. There will be no time for anything else. Work, holidays, hobbies and social life must all be abandoned for the time being.

2. Choose a room in which you intend to give pills to your cat. The room in which you intend to give pills to your cat will be known as the 'treatment room'.

3. This room must be made secure and cat proof. Cat proofing a room can best be compared to waterproofing the hull of a ship. It is crucial but difficult.

4. Hire a locksmith to put strong new locks on all doors and windows leading in or out of the treatment room. Experience shows that seven lever locks should be used. All doors and windows must be thoroughly locked when the treatment room is in use.

5. Block all gaps under doors. Do not dismiss small spaces as of no consequence. An angry or desperate cat can squeeze through a space too small to accommodate an anorexic mouse.

6. Purchase two pairs of very thick gloves. It is my experience that gauntlets are better than gloves since they provide some protection for the wrists and lower forearms. The sort of heavy duty gauntlets which were favoured by motor cyclists in the 1950's are generally suitable.

7. Replenish your domestic first aid kit. You will need sticking plasters, liquid antiseptic and suture materials. As a rule of thumb I recommend buying two boxes of plasters and a bottle of liquid antiseptic for every day you intend to be giving pills to your cat. You will also need plenty of bandages, cloths and towels. A good supply of heavy duty absorbent paper towels will also be useful for mopping up pools of blood. (Don't worry: this will not be your cat's blood.)

8. Purchase a large supply of cat food and cat litter. A cat who is going to take pills must not be let out of the house until the course has been completed.

9. Contact your local hospital. Make sure they have a supply of compatible blood available. (The blood will, of course, be for you, not the cat.)

10. Make sure that your GP is on stand-by.

11. Visit your solicitor and check that your will is up-to-date.

12. Do not, under any circumstances, allow the vet to prescribe pills which need to be given more than three times a day. Giving a pill to a cat takes at least 8 hours (including a modest recovery period afterwards) and so giving pills at six hourly intervals is a physical impossibility.

13. Do not try to give a pill to a cat by yourself – i.e. without help. You will need at least two assistants if you are to give a pill to a cat successfully. If more assistants are available this will be a bonus. (There is, however, a limit to the optimum number of assistants. I have found that when there are more than 15 assistants gathered around one cat, there may be too many hands and too little cat available.)

14. Make sure that all your assistants have signed liability waivers, taking full responsibility for whatever may happen to them and excusing both you and your cat from legal action. You, in turn, should sign a document promising not to sue them should their actions result in damage to your furniture, home or person.

15. When the vet provides you with a supply of pills, ask for 'spares'. (This number is obtained by multiplying the number required by 6.5. The figure of 6.5 is a result of much experience. In practice this means that if, for example, the vet has prescribed 21 pills for your cat you should ask for 137 pills to be dispensed. (Your vet may agree to purchase back from you any pills which have not been used and which have not been chewed, sucked or spat out. Sticky pills which are covered with bits of blood and carpet have an almost negligible resale value.)

16. When preparing to give a pill to a cat you should wear the toughest, strongest clothing you can find. You should choose clothing which covers all areas of your body. Climbers and other outdoor enthusiasts recommend using several layers of thin clothing to keep out cold winds. To protect your skin from an angry cat's claws I recommend that you follow this philosophy but instead of choosing *thin* clothing you should select *thick* clothing. Do not leave legs, arms or other areas uncovered. Under some circumstances (such as when dealing with a cat who has been given pills on previous occasions) it might be wise to wear a motor cyclist's helmet, complete with visor.

Harold: "I've bought you a fish for Christmas."
Gilbert: "A fish? What a surprise! How wonderful. However did you guess?"

17. The first assistant should lock you, the cat and your second assistant into the treatment room. (Any other assistants should be locked in with you). You should be dressed appropriately. You should take with you: the pills, your first aid kit, two pairs of gauntlets (one pair for you and one for your second assistant), a rubbish bin into which you can toss soggy tablets, as many absorbent paper towels as you can carry, your best bathroom towels, a stepladder high enough to reach the highest point in the room, and a fully-charged mobile telephone. The first assistant should be given instructions that he/she is not to open the treatment room door until you and the second assistant both confirm that you are satisfied that the pill has been taken. The first assistant will then open the door and let you (but not the cat) out.

18. After you have been locked in the treatment room with your second assistant you should expect to spend fifteen minutes trying to find the cat. It will eventually dawn on you that although you remembered everything else you forgot to take the cat into the room with you. Do not feel embarrassed about this; it happens so often that I now regard it as part of the official plan. It will take another twenty minutes to persuade your first assistant to open the door and let you out so that you can search for the cat.

19. By now the cat will, of course, know that something is up. Consequently, searching for the cat will take between one and two hours. (If someone has left the back door open or forgotten to block off the cat flap it could take considerably longer than this.) By the time you have found the cat you and your assistants will be exhausted. You will, of course, have forgotten your gauntlets and you will have received a number of wounds to your hands and forearms. There will be no time for a cup of tea and a sit down. The pill must be given and the clock is ticking. So you must go back to the treatment room. You and your second assistant must get yourselves locked in again. This time try to remember to take the cat with you.

20. By trial and error I have decided that the best way to carry out the next part of the procedure is for one person to hold the cat on the

ground (firmly but gently) while the other opens the cat's jaws, slips the pill between the cat's clenched teeth and then holds the cat's jaws clenched tight until the cat has swallowed. The person holding the cat can wear gauntlets. The person holding the pill cannot. It is physically impossible to hold and control a pill while wearing thick gloves of any kind. You will find that although this scenario sounds easy to manage it is not. Unless you have at least 35 years experience it is not possible to hold a cat firmly and gently at the same time. You can do one or you can do the other. Most people end up doing neither with the result that in the blink of an eye the cat will be sitting washing itself on the pelmet, on top of the bookcase or in some other impossible-to-reach spot.

21. At this point it is important to panic. Remaining calm is all very well in its place but remaining calm will not make you feel any better about things. Indeed, in my experience, making an effort to remain calm may result in your blood pressure rising to an

"We're going on a demonstration," said Rupert. "Would you like to come?"
"I don't know," replied Sooty. "What are you demonstrating about?"
"We're not demonstrating <u>about</u> anything," said Rupert. "We're demonstrating our beauty, style and grace."
"Oh right," said Sooty. "Well I'll certainly join you then."

unsafe level. So have a little panic. I find that dancing around the room and tearing at my hair helps. After a couple of minutes of this I like to sit down on the floor, hold my head in my hands and sob quietly for a while. You might like to do the same. When you and your assistant have finished panicking you will probably find that the cat has finished washing and has fallen asleep on its perch.

22. Using the stepladder which you thoughtfully brought with you, the next step is to retrieve the cat from its perch. Once you've done this you can once again try to give a pill to your cat.

23. Remember that cats are very good at pretending to take tablets. When you are relaxed and celebrating, convinced that you have given your cat a pill, you will probably find that you have celebrated prematurely. I remember the first time this happened to me. After hours of effort, I was finally convinced that my cat Alice had swallowed a pill which I had managed to cram into her mouth. I had had a bath, put plasters on the largest scratches, poured myself a large malt whisky and sunk into an armchair. I then noticed the pill which Alice had spat out. It was lying in the middle of the carpet. I still don't know how she did this. But all cats can do it. After pretending to swallow a pill a cat will eat a large meal, yawn and *then* spit out the pill. I am convinced that cats have a secret pouch (which vets don't know about) built inside their mouths. This pouch is just big enough to hide a pill. When the cat is given a pill he or she tucks it into the pouch. Later, when you're relaxing and feeling smug he or she will take the pill out of the pouch and spit it out on the carpet.

24. Telephone the vet. Ask him if the medication is really necessary. If he says it is ask him to come round to your house and give your cat his medication by injection. Tell him that you will pay whatever he wants. (Every vet I have ever known has lived in a huge house, driven a massively expensive car and needed at least three wives to wear all the jewellery.)

Catalina, known to her friends as Gypsy, was the seventh kitten of a seventh kitten and had something of a reputation as a tail reader. Cats came from several gardens away to have their tails read by her. Catalina's normal fee for this was a freshly caught mouse.

Chapter Seven

Cats in Films

True cat lovers always notice the cats in films – even when the cats aren't scene stealing. (Scene stealing is something most thespian felines are very good at). If I'm watching a movie with Donna Antoinette she will always notice the cats, even if they are in the background and of no real importance to the development of the plot. If we are watching a video or DVD the chances are that we will just rewind and watch the bit with the cat in until it's time to go to bed. The rest of the film will be ignored and forgotten.

Once, in a cinema in Carmarthen, Donna Antoinette leapt up, ran to the back of the cinema and asked the projectionist to rewind the film and reshow the part in which a cat had appeared. To my surprise the projectionist obliged. The film was *Dr No*. I remember thinking how odd it was that those members of the audience who didn't share our affection for cats should show their disapproval by making cat-calls.

I digress.

Here, for cat lovers who also like films, is a list of some of the films in which cats make memorable appearances, either in the story or the title, though not always both.

I have omitted films such as *The Wrong Box*, *Torture Garden* and *A Walk on the Wild Side* in which cats make significant walk on appearances but do not have starring roles. I have, of course, also omitted films in which cats have stroll-on roles, are present coincidentally or can be spotted in the background only because the despairing and hairless director eventually gave up trying to get them out of camera shot.

1. *Breakfast at Tiffany's* (1961)
Cat (played by Orangey) starred with Audrey Hepburn, playing Holly Golightly. Even people who don't love cats admit that Orangey steals the film from the delightful Ms Hepburn and from everyone else in the movie.

2. *The Three Lives of Thomasina* (1963)
A girl in a Scottish village treats animals by giving them love. The film, which is based on the novel by Paul Gallico, stars Susan Hampshire and the greatest James Bond who never was, Patrick McGoohan. If you haven't seen it, this is well worth seeing.

3. *That Darn Cat!* (1965)
The film stars Hayley Mills, Dean Jones and Syn (a Siamese) who played the title role.

4. *That Darn Cat* (1997)
A remake of the 1965 film. Once again a girl solves a mystery with the aid of a cat.

5. *Catlow* (1971)
An outlaw has problems recovering his hidden gold. Starring a furless Yul Brynner and no cats that I can remember.

6. *The Cat's Paw* (1936)
One of the films written by and starring Harold Lloyd before he became a slapstick star. Nothing much to do with cats but a nice title.

7. *The Cat's Meow* (2001)
A murder mystery starring Kirsten Dunst and Cary Elwes.

8. *Gay Purr-ee* (1962)
The first full length film to feature a cat as the star. The cat with the big trailer was called Mewsette and in the film the cat's voice was provided by Judy Garland.

Elsie liked to take the cat for a walk, but Tiddles didn't like to get his feet dirty

The Lancashire cat and the Cheshire cat are almost indistinguishable. But experts claim there is a discernible difference.

9. *The Cat and the Canary* (1927)
Laura LaPlante, Creighton Hale and Forrest Stanley star in a comedy horror film in which relatives meet in a mansion for the reading of a will. The first heir proves to be insane and after much to-do the eventual heir turns out to be a cat.

10. *The Cat Creeps* (1930)
Starring Helen Twelvetrees, Raymond Hacket and Neil Hamilton. This is a revised version of the 1927 film *The Cat and the Canary* – this time with sound.

11. *The Cat and the Canary* (1939)
In this version, starring Bob Hope and Paulette Goddard, there is a scary housekeeper who always has the eventual heir (a black cat) by her side. As you might guess from the presence of Bob Hope, not always to be taken entirely seriously.

12. *The Cat Creeps* (1946)
Nothing whatsoever to do with the other film with the same title. Starring Noah Beery Jr (who later became Jim Rockford's father in The Rockford Files) and a black cat which solves murders in its spare time.

13. *The Cat and the Canary* (1979)
Honor Blackman and Edward Fox starring in a loose adaptation of the original stage play.

14. *The Cat Ate the Parakeet* (1972)
For once the title says it all. This is a film about a parakeet which is eaten by a cat. A whole darned film about a parakeet which is eaten by a cat!

15. *Cat Ballou* (1965)
Comedy western starring Jane Fonda and Lee Marvin. Nothing much to do with cats.

16. *The Cat Gang* (1959)
A gang of children captures a band of smugglers.

17. *Cat Girl* (1957)
A horror movie starring a woman who thinks she has a curse which will turn her soul into a leopard.

18. *The Cat from Outer Space* (1978)
Starring Sandy Duncan, Harry Morgan, Roddy McDowall. An alien cat lands on earth and needs help in repairing his spacecraft so that he can get back home. (I wish I'd been there when the writer pitched the idea to the producer.)

19. *Cat People* (1942)
Simone Simon, Kent Smith and Elizabeth Russell star in a film based on a Serbian legend about women who, when they becomes jealous, change into wild cats.

20. *Cat People* (1982)
Nastassja Kinski and Malcolm McDowell in a rough remake of the 1942 version of the same story. David Bowie wrote the music and lyrics.

21. *The Cat* (1959)
Starring Francoise Arnoul. A Parisian widow is recruited into the French Resistance and falls in love with a German officer.

22. *Catman of Paris* (1946)
An amnesia victim may be the mad killer strolling the streets of Paris. Or, then again, he may not. Starring Carl Esmond.

23. *Cats and Dogs* (2001)
A Persian cat's scheme to take over the world is foiled by a puppy. Starring Jeff Goldblum and the voices of a host of stars.

24. *Cat's Eye* (1985)
Three horror stories linked by a cat. Starring Drew Barrymore and James Woods.

25. *The Cat* (1966)
Roger Perry and Peggy Ann Garner in a film about a boy who runs away to find his neighbour's pet wildcat. The boy finds the cat then witnesses a murder. The wildcat saves the boy from the murderer.

26. *The Cat* (1971)
Jean Gabin and Simone Signoret. A husband and wife fall out of love and grow to loathe one another. Great. Not a film to watch if you're feeling slightly miserable.

27. *Catwoman* (2004)
An artist who is left for dead by a bunch of thugs is transformed into a woman with the physical skills and moral sense of a cat. The cat is played by Halle Berry.

'People were afraid to approach me; when they did, they did it with the utmost respect and kindness,' said Ms Berry afterwards. 'They measured their words and they were really different around me when I had the cat suit on.'

28. *The Black Cat* (1934)
A horror movie, starring both Boris Karloff and Bela Lugosi. The film is named after the Edgar Allan Poe story but has nothing much to do with it. Lugosi's character has an all-consuming horror of cats.

"It's a horror film ..."

29. *The Black Cat* (1941)
Starring Basil Rathbone (better known as the 'original' Sherlock Holmes), Bela Lugosi and Broderick Crawford. A group of avaricious relatives sit around waiting for their aunt to die so that they can collect their inheritances. One of them murders the aunt. They then discover that her will stipulates that the money won't be released until all the cats in her house have died. So the cats start dying.

30. *The Black Cat* (1966)
Starring Robert Frost and Robyn Baker. This version really is based on the Poe story. A man kills a black cat because he thinks it is a reincarnation of his father. He walls up the cat, which is called Phito, with the corpse of his wife.

31. *The Cat and Mouse* (1958)
Starring Lee Patterson, Victor Maddern and Ann Sears this isn't a Tom and Jerry film but a movie about a girl who is held hostage by men who want to recover jewels her father has stolen.

32. *Cat and Mouse* (1974)
Kirk Douglas plays a teacher who takes vengeance on his wife. I can't remember why and don't much care.

33. *Cat and Mouse* (1975)
A French film starring Michele Morgan, Serge Reggiani and Philippe Leotard. A detective investigates the murder of a wealthy philanderer.

34. *Cat Women of the Moon* (1953)
Starring Sonny Tufts, Victor Play and a lot of glamour girls. American spacemen land on the moon and meet a race of telepathic cat women in sexy black leotards.

35. *The Incredible Journey* (1963)
Two dogs and a cat who are separated from their Uprights, escape and travel 250 miles to get home. From a book by Sheila Burnford.

Tiddles couldn't fly but he could twist himself into some very impressive positions – especially when trying to catch butterflies.

Picasso's cat admires a portrait of himself done by his Master.

36. *The Goldwyn Follies* (1938)
Starring Kenny Baker and the Ritz Brothers. In the film the Ritz
Brothers are joined by hundreds of cats singing 'Hey Pussy'.

37. *The Blue Bird* (1940)
Starring Shirley Temple. A sleek black cat called Tylette is humanised
into Gale Sondergaard.

38. *The Tomb of Ligeia* (1964)
A Victorian husband turns his dead wife into a cat. Written by Robert
Towne from a story by Edgar Allan Poe and directed by Roger Corman.
Starring Vincent Price and Elizabeth Shepherd.

The hunt

39. *Eye of the Cat* (1969)
A young man who hates cats goes to stay with his aunt. Unfortunately for him she has a house full of cats. Written by Joseph Stefano (who wrote *Psycho*). Starring Michael Sarrazin and Gayle Hunnicutt

40. *The Cat and the Fiddle* (1933)
A musical comedy starring Jeanette MacDonald and Ramon Novarro.

Chapter Eight

A Tour Of Vernon Coleman's Catland

"The one at the top took me three hours to catch. I found him in the cellar and eventually finished him off in the spare bedroom."

William and Agnes found that sleepy cats made very useful fashion accessories when the weather was cold.

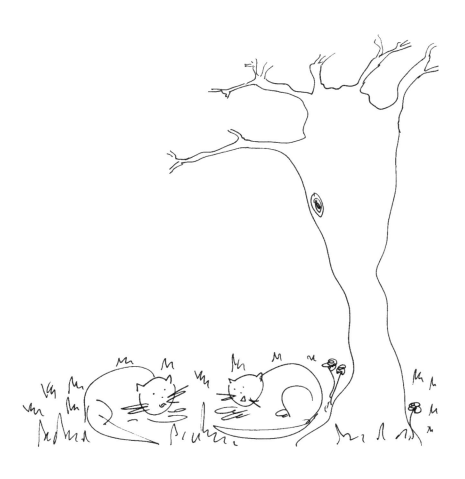

"On the whole," said Sooty, "I would rather be lying in the sun."
"But we are!" said George.
"Oh," said Sooty. "Are we? I was having such a good time I thought I must be dreaming."

Tiddles had a wonderful Christmas. He went for long walks in the snow. He chased mice in an old barn. He ran through sunlit meadows chasing butterflies. And all the time he lay in front of the fire dreaming.

She: "Do you think she's comfortable?"
He: "I'm sure she is."
She: "Maybe I'll just give her one more cushion."

"I suppose we'd better call the fire brigade."
"No need. He'll come down when he's hungry."

"How do I get to the other side?"

"You're on the other side."

"Keyboards are very comfortable," thought Tiddles. "They mould themselves to your shape very nicely."

1st kitten: *"You ask her."*

2nd kitten: *"No. You ask her."*

1st kitten: *"OK. Excuse me, missus Queen but do you take that off
 when you go mousing?"*

*"I'll go for a long brisk walk every Sunday," Tiddles told his friends.
"It helps me keep fit."*

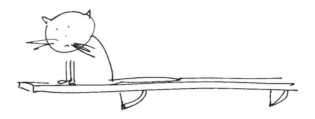

Poppy: "Why are you looking so glum?"

Nippy: "There isn't anything left to knock off. Suddenly, life seems worthless and without purpose."

Poppy: "Cheer up! The Uprights will buy more ornaments tomorrow."

Dottie loved cats and even had a cat-shaped suitcase. It wasn't very practical, but Dottie didn't care about that.

"You go on ahead."

"That's not quite
what I meant."

Tiddles enjoyed being in show business.
"I like being admired by strangers," he said.
"I think it must be in my blood."

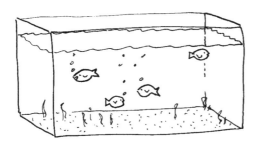 

*"I've worked out that if we both drink solidly for nine hours
we can get all the fish."*

You wait for hours and then two come along at the same time.

Tiddles and Tiddlelina had spent a busy morning doing nothing and had decided that they needed a good rest. After a great deal of thought, a lengthy appraisal of the various possibilities, a number of meetings, advice from various official bodies and a considerable amount of soul searching they decided to go to sleep on a pile of freshly laundered towels in the airing cupboard.

Tiddles' favourite things to do No 1

Window Shopping

Tiddles' favourite things to do No 2

A night out on the tiles with a chum.

Tiddles' favourite things to do No 3

Having friends round by for tea.

Tiddles' favourite things to do No 4

Moving into a new home.

Tiddles' favourite things to do No 5

Finding a comfortable-looking lap.

Tiddles had a big win on the Premium Bonds.
"The winnings make a very comfortable bed," he said, in a prepared
statement to the press.

Chapter Nine

The Things People Say About Cats...

No animal in the world has attracted as much wonderful prose or excellent poetry as the cat.

Here, collected from books in numerous languages, are some of my favourite quotes about kittens and cats.

'The cat doesn't caress us; he uses us to caress himself.'

Rivarol

'Man is civilised to the extent that he understands the cat.'

Jean Cocteau

'Mr Leonard, a very intelligent friend of mine, saw a cat catch a trout, by darting upon it in a deep clear water, at the mill at Weaford, near Lichfield. The cat belonged to Mr Stanley, who had often seen her catch fish in the same manner in summer, when the mill-pool was drawn so low that the fish could be seen. I have heard of other cats taking fish in shallow water, as they stood on the bank. This seems to be a natural method of taking their prey, usually lost by domestication, though they all retain a strong relish for fish.'

Charles Darwin

'Few animals display their mood via facial expressions as distinctly as the cat.'

Konrad Lorenz

'There are always cats watching and waiting, malicious and unfaithful, with paws of velvet.'

Le Rochefourcauld

'The little cat pretends that the piece of paper is a mouse. He touches is lightly, afraid that he might otherwise destroy the illusion.'

Joseph Joubert

'I have an adorable white mistress called Snowy. She's a pure bred cat, pretty, and I kiss her every day on her pink nose. She erases my verse with her tail, walking on my table as I write.'

Stéphane Mellarmé

'If it be true that nations have the cats they deserve, then the English people deserve well of cats, for there are none so prosperous or so friendly in the world.'

Hilaire Belloc

'A heaven without cats would, of course, be deserted for a hell with them.'

Carl Van Vechten

'Man has a wonderful life. He has hands to stroke the fur of cats.'

Theophile Gautier

'The superiority of the cat over the dog is that there isn't a police cat.'

Jean Cocteau

'You can't own a cat. The best you can do is be partners.'

Harry Swanson

'What I admire in the cat is his independent character.'

Francois-René de Chateaubriand

'A Gentleman Cat does not mew except in extremity. He makes his wishes known and waits.'

May Sarton

'The idea of peace is a sitting cat.'

Jules Renard

'On waking up I see that the cat on the chair is looking at me fixedly, immobile. He has, perhaps, spent the night in this position.'

Fernando Arrabal

'Way down deep, we're all motivated by the same urges. Cats have the courage to live by them.'

Jim Davis

'Cats are a mysterious kind of folk. There is more passing in their minds than we are aware of.'

Sir Walter Scott

'The cat is a guest and not a plaything.'

Collette

'The cat is at our side a warm memory; hair, whiskers and purring of a lost paradise.'

Leonor Fini

Malcolm the Mouse and Korky the Cat were good friends and met every Tuesday and Thursday for a little cheese, some milk and a chat. Their cheese and milk parties were, indeed, quite the talk of the town where they lived.

'The cat is, above all things, a dramatist.'

Margaret Benson

'Every waking moment was precious to her; in it she would find something useful to do – and if she ran out of material and couldn't find anything else to do she would have kittens.'

Mark Twain, writing about his cat, Sour Mash

'The three animals that waste most time over their toilet are cats, flies and women.'

C. H. Ross

'Confront a child, a puppy, and a kitten with a sudden danger; the child will turn instinctively for assistance, the puppy will grovel in abject submission, the kitten will brace its tiny body for a frantic resistance.'

Saki

'You can keep a dog; but it is the cat who keeps people, because cats find humans useful domestic animals.'

George Mikes

'From time to time, newspapers print stories about some elderly widow who died and left her entire estate, valued at £3,200,000, to her cat, Fluffkins. Cats read these stories too, and are always plotting to get named as beneficiaries in their owners' wills. Did you ever wonder where your cat goes when it wanders off for several hours? It meets with other cats in estate-planning seminars. I just thought you should know.'

Dave Barry

'You must set down all the rules to your cat at the beginning of your relationship. You cannot add rules as you go along. Once these rules are set, you must never, under any circumstances, break any of them. Dare to break a rule, and you will never live it down. Trust me.'

Kathy Young

'Cats exercise a magic influence upon highly developed men of intellect. This is why these long-tailed Graces of the animal kingdom, these adorable, scintillating electric batteries have been the favourite animal of a Mohammed, Cardinal Richelieu, Crebillon, Rousseau, Wieland.'

Leopold von Sacher-Masoch

'Kittens are born with their eyes shut. They open them in about six days, take a look around, then close them again for the better part of their lives.'

Stephen Baker

'My admirable cat has never denied herself one of the little pleasures of life.'

Oswald Barron

'Dogs believe they are human. Cats believe they are God.'

Jeff Valdez

'The beauty and subtlety of cats commended them, even in the darkest days, to intelligent and discriminating people.'

Olivia Manning

'The cat is far more particular and exacting in its choice of friends and confidants than the dog.'

Charles Platt

'Cats didn't start out as mousers...I postulate that cats started as psychic companions, as Familiars, and have never deviated from this function.'

William S. Burroughs

'There is no snooze button on a cat who wants breakfast.'

Anon

'Because of their aloofness, the secret of getting the most out of cats is numbers. I am owned by six of them, so that when I really need a cuddle, at least one cat will hopefully be in the mood to oblige.'

Mira Bar-Hillel

'Cats are kindly masters, just so long as you remember your place.'

Paul Gray

'Everybody knows that a writer with a cat at his elbow is the very picture of creativeness.'

Maurice Wiggin

'Thousands of years ago, cats were worshipped as gods. Cats have never forgotten this.'

Anon

'All people who keep cats, and are in the habit of nursing them, do not suffer from those petty little ailments which all flesh is heir to, viz., nervous complaints of a minor sort. Hysteria and rheumatism, too, are unknown, and all lovers of 'pussy' are of the sweetest temperament.'

Louis Wain

"I feel hungry," said Samson
"You don't look it," thought Tiddles

'If you are worthy of its affection, a cat will be your friend, but never your slave.'

Theophile Gautier

'Every cat lover knows that a cat cannot be induced, either by reason or by affection, to act in accordance with any wishes save its own.'

Helen M. Winslow

'Even when a kitten is quiet, nothing can be more amusing. The little crouching creature with its shut eyes has such a knowing, touch-me-not air. Its head hanging as though overwhelmed with sleep, its stretched-out paws, its dainty little nose, all seem to say, 'Don't wake me. I am so happy!' A sleeping kitten is the image of perfect beatitude.

Champfleury

'Cats are connoisseurs of comfort.'

James Herriot

1st cat: *"Why do Uprights worry so much?"*
2nd cat: *"I don't know. But I don't suppose there's much point in worrying about it.*

'Cats seem to go on the principle that it never does any harm to ask for what you want.'

Joseph Wood Krutch

'If there is one spot of sun spilling onto the floor, a cat will find it and soak it up.'

Joan Asper McIntosh

'He lies there, purring and dreaming, shifting his limbs now and then in an ecstasy of cushioned comfort. He seems the incarnation of everything soft and silky and velvety...'

Saki (Hector Hugh Munro)

'Recognise the great truth, that the only and true owner of the house is the cat, and perhaps for the reason that he is the only one to enjoy and live in the whole house, from the studio to the larder, from the dining room to the roof...from the darkness under the stairs to the gardens where he climbs the trees....he goes in every place inaccessible to man.'

Giovanni Rajberti

'The clever cat eats cheese and breathes down rat holes with baited breath.'

W.C. Fields

'It's really the cat's house. I just pay the mortgage.'

Anon

'There can be no doubt that cats know a great deal more than they choose to tell us.'

Philip Gilbert Hamerton

'As anyone who has ever been around a cat for any length of time well knows, cats have enormous patience with the limitations of the human kind.'

Cleveland Amory

'Of all God's creatures there is only one that cannot be made the slave of the lash. That one is the cat.'

Mark Twain

'I am one of the most fanatical cat lovers in the business.'

Raymond Chandler

'I wish I could write as mysterious as a cat.'

Edgar Allan Poe

'Cats are smarter than dogs. You can't get eight cats to pull a sled through snow.'

Jeff Valdez

'Last year a team of scientists published the results of an extensive study of cat language. They determined that although cats may demonstrate a wide variety of vocalisations, they actually only have two phrases that are translatable into human terms: 1. Hurry up with that food. 2. Everything here is mine.

Anon

Andy: "I've written a musical called "Uprights!"

'The difference between a cat and a dog. A dog thinks: 'They feed me, they shelter me, they love me, they must be gods.' A cat thinks: 'They feed me, they shelter me, they love me, I must be god.'

Anon

'I believe cats to be spirits come to earth. A cat, I am sure, could walk on a cloud without coming through.'

Jules Verne

'Cats are the ultimate narcissists. You can tell this because of all the time they spend on personal grooming. Dogs aren't like this. A dog's idea of personal grooming is to roll in a dead fish.'

James Gorman

'My relationship with my cats has saved me from a deadly, pervasive ignorance.'

William S Burroughs

'When dogs leap on to your bed, it's because they adore being with you. When cats leap on to your bed, it's because they adore your bed.'

Alisha Everett

'A great treat for pussy, when she is a little bit seedy – of a morning, perhaps, after having been on the spree occasionally – is a saucer of nice creamy milk, made warm with water, and slightly sweetened with sugar. It sets her all to rights straight away, and you will not find her ungrateful for such kindness.'

W. Gordon Stables

'Cat lovers can readily be identified. Their clothes always look old and well used. Their sheets look like bath towels, and their bath towels look like a collection of knitting mistakes.'

Eric Gurney

'A cat doesn't know what it wants and wants more of it.'

Richard Hexem

'A cat I find...is an easier companion than a dog. A cat's sense of independence also enables oneself to be independent.'

Derek Tangye

'To bathe a cat takes brute force, perseverance, courage of conviction – and a cat. The last ingredient is usually the hardest to come by.'

Stephen Baker

'Cats do not need to be shown how to have a good time, for they are unfailingly ingenious in that respect.'

James Mason

'Okay, cats will never bring you pictures they've drawn in school, but they may give you a dead mouse. What parent could resist that gift?'

Terri L. Haney

'Do our cats name us? My former husband swore that Humphrey and Dolly and Beau Blossom called me The Big Hamburger.'

Eleanora Walker

'The more cats you have, the longer you live.'

Charles Bukowski

'Cats always know whether people like or dislike them. They do not always care enough to do anything about it.'

Winifred Carriere

Cats are just little hair factories.'

Jim Davis

'An ordinary kitten will ask more questions than any five-year-old boy.'

Carl Van Vechten

'There are two kinds of fidelity, that of dogs and that of cats; you, gentlemen, have the fidelity of cats, who never leave the house.'

Napoleon Bonaparte (to those who met him on his return from Elba)

'It is said that cats are untrainable. That is not totally accurate. Appearances to the contrary, cats do pay attention to the instructions they receive. They listen closely to what you have to say and sometimes even wait for you to finish your sentence. They understand plain English as well as anybody. How else would it be possible for them to so uncannily do just the opposite?'

Stephen Baker

'A cat has absolute emotional honesty: human beings, for one reason or another may hide their feelings, but a cat does not.'

Ernest Hemingway

'A Gentleman Cat has an immaculate shirt front and paws at all times.'

May Sarton

'Apparently, through scientific research, it has been determined that a cat's affection gland is stimulated by snoring, thus explaining my cat's uncontrollable urge to rub against my face at 2 am.'

Terri L Haney

'A mouse in the paws is worth two in the pantry.'

Louis Wain

'Cats instinctively know the precise moment their owners will awaken...then they awaken them ten minutes sooner.'

Jim Davis

'How do cats decide when to jump suddenly up from where they were sitting comfortably, curled up, and dash madly around the room, knocking over everything they encounter?'

Andrew Koenig

'And Cats as well as Kings like flattery.'

Robert Southey

'The cat does not offer services. The cat offers itself.'

William S. Burroughs

'Dogs come when they're called; cats take a message and get back to you later.'

Mary Bly

'I gave my cat a bath the other day. He sat there, he enjoyed it, it was fun for me. The fur would stick to my tongue, but other than that...'

Steve Martin

'Cats do not think that they are little people. They think that we are big cats. This influences their behaviour in many ways.'

Anon

"Have you perhaps thought of cutting him down to, say, just twelve meals a day?"

'The playful kitten with its pretty tigerish gambol is infinitely more amusing than half the people one is obliged to live with in the world.'

Lady Sydney Morgan

'God invented the cat so that man would have a tiger to caress.'

Victor Hugo

'Do not meddle in the affairs of cats, for they are subtle and they will pee on your computer.'

Bruce Graham

'A computer and a cat are somewhat alike: they both purr and like to be stroked, and spend a lot of the day motionless. They also have secrets they don't necessarily share.'

John Updike

'Cats are rather delicate creatures and they are subject to a good many ailments, but I never heard of one who suffered from insomnia.'

Joseph Wood Krutch

'There has never been a skeleton of a cat found in a tree; therefore, they must come down on their own.'

Old American saying

'The best mousetrap ever invented: a cat.'

Evan Esar

'There are many intelligent species in the universe. They are all owned by cats.'

Anon

'A Gentleman Cat approaches food slowly, however hungry he may be, and decides at least three feet away whether it is Good, Fair, Passable or Unworthy. If Unworthy, he pretends to scratch earth over it.'

May Sarton

'The only self-cleaning thing in this kitchen is the cat.'

Anon

'Cats are intended to teach us that not everything in nature has a purpose.'

Garrison Keillor

'When addressed, a Gentleman Cat does not move a muscle. He looks as if he hadn't heard.'

May Sarton

'People who hate cats will come back as mice in their next life.'

Faith Resnick

'The way to keep a cat is to try to chase it away.'

E.W. Howe

'A Gentleman Cat gives thanks for a Worthy meal, by licking the plate so clean that a person might think it had been washed.'

May Sarton

'I've never understood why women love cats. Cats are independent, they don't listen, they don't come in when you call, they like to stay out all night, and when they're home they like to be left alone and sleep. In other words, every quality that women hate in a man, they love in a cat.'

Jay Leno

'A creature that never cries over spilt milk: a cat.'

Evan Esar

'There is a ridiculous idea that dogs are superior to cats because cats cannot be trained. A cat will not jump into a lake and bring back a stick. Would you?'

Robert Stearns

'Most cats have trained their owners. When the cat meows before the refrigerator, the owner obediently opens the door and feeds the cat. When it meows at the back door, the owner is trained to let the cat out.'

Leon F. Whitney

'Cats, like cars, tend to get stolen, scratched and weather-worn if parked outside night after night.'

David Taylor

'A Gentleman Cat allows no constraint of his person, even loving constraint.'

May Sarton

'The cat: an animal that's so unpredictable, you can never tell in advance how it will ignore you the next time.'

Evan Esar

"My name is Alfie and I'm a mouseaholic."

'The cat appears to have feelings only for himself, loves only conditionally, and enters into relations with people only to abuse them.'

George Louis Leclerc de Buffon

'A Gentleman Cat takes no interest in other people's affairs, unless he is directly concerned.'

May Sarton

'Those who'll play with cats must expect to be scratched.'

Miguel de Cervantes

'A cat is a soft, indestructible automaton provided by nature to be kicked when things go wrong in the domestic circle.'

Ambrose Bierce (writing in his Devil's Dictionary*)*

'I found out why cats drink out of the toilet. My mother told me it's because the water's cold in there. And I'm like: How did my mother know that?'

Wendy Liebman

Tiddles: "You're looking very smart today."
Tiddlelina: "I've had my tail done."
Tiddles: "Are you going somewhere special?"
Tiddlelina: "Just to see you."

'Even overweight cats instinctively know the cardinal rule: when fat, arrange yourself in slim poses.'

John Weitz

'If a dog jumps into your lap, it is because he is fond of you; but if a cat does the same thing, it is because your lap is warmer.'

Alfred North Whitehead

'It is as easy to hold quicksilver between your finger and thumb as to keep a cat who means to escape.'

Andrew Lang

'To respect the cat is the beginning of the aesthetic sense.'

Erasmus Darwin

'Like a graceful vase, a cat, even when motionless, seems to flow.'

George Will

'With their qualities of cleanliness, discretion, affection, patience, dignity and courage, how many of us, I ask you, would be capable of being cats.'

Fernand Mery

'Disdain is an important weapon in the armoury of the pet cat.'

Paul Gallico

'Cats may sense early on that you don't like paw prints on your butter, but they will jump on to any surface in the home as long as no one sees it happen.'

Kathy Young

'A kitten is chiefly remarkable for rushing about like mad at nothing whatever, and generally stopping before it gets there.'

Agnes Repplier

'The tail, in cats, is the principle organ of emotional expression.'

Aldous Huxley

'A kitten is so flexible that she is almost double; the hind part is equivalent to another kitten with which the forepart plays. She does not discover that her tail belongs to her until you tread on it.'

Henry David Thoreau

'Cats are a mysterious kind of folk. There is more passing in their minds than we are aware of.'

Sir Walter Scott

'Do you know why Cats always wash themselves after a meal? A Cat caught a sparrow, and was about to devour it, but the sparrow said: 'No gentleman eats till he has first washed his face.' The Cat, struck with this remark, set the sparrow down, and began to wash his face with his paw, but the sparrow flew away. This vexed Pussy extremely, and he said: 'As long as I live I will eat first and wash my face afterwards.'

C. H. Ross

'The idea, to a cat, that someone else owns him is ludicrous.'

Jeffrey Moussaieff Masson

'Everything a cat is and does physically is to me beautiful, lovely, stimulating, soothing, attractive and an enchantment.'

Paul Gallico

'Her function is to sit and be admired.'

Georgina Stickland Gates

'Conscious of her high lineage, the Cat understands and accepts the responsibilities that attach to it. She knows what she owes to herself, to her rank, to the Royal Idea. Therefore it is you who must be the courtier.'

The Yellow Book, *July 1896*

'I'm used to dogs. When you leave them in the morning, they stick their nose in the door crack and stand there like a portrait until you turn the key eight hours later. A cat would never put up with that kind of rejection.'

Erma Bombeck

'Anyone who considers protocol unimportant has never dealt with a cat.'

Robert A.Heinlein

'One cannot be too careful not to irritate or offend them.'

Queen Elizabeth of Rumania

'Anybody, but anybody, any lout, any half-wit, any scruffy, self-centred moron, can command the affection and the servile obedience of a dog, but it takes intelligence and understanding...to win the affection of a cat.'

Beverly Nichols

'The cat is such a perfect symbol of beauty and superiority that it seems scarcely possible for any true aesthete and civilised cynic to do other than worship it.'

H. P. Lovecraft

'All you have to remember is Rule 1: when in doubt, wash.'
Paul Gallico

'You can keep a dog; but it is the cat who keeps people, because cats find humans useful domestic animals.'

George Mikes

'As you carefully prepared Ginger's fifth tiger prawn, do you ever feel that somebody somewhere is taking advantage.'

Vicky Halls

'There are records of Cats that raised the knocker on the centre of the outer door, and showed obvious signs of importance and dignity when the housemaid came and let them in.'

Charles Platt

'Petting a purring cat accomplishes something in the soul that cannot be described.'

Jo Kittinger

'My cats don't mind my shortcomings, and I don't think that they have any.'

Bruce Marshall

"I'm not fat," said Marvin. "I'm big furred."

'A happy arrangement: many people prefer cats to other people, and many cats prefer people to other cats.'

Mason Cooley

'Although the love of my cats is not, like choucroute in French restaurants, constantly on top, at least I can love them at all hours.'

Bruce Marshall

'Ignorant people think it's the noise which fighting cats make that is so aggravating, but it ain't so; it's the disgusting grammar they use.'

Mark Twain

'When I play with my cat, who knows whether I do not make her more sport than she makes me? We mutually divert one another with our play.'

Montaigne

'Are we as its devotees, hoping that some of this marvel and mystery will rub off on us?'

Paul Gallico

'Our house they say; and mine, the cat declares...
And spreads his golden fleece upon the chairs...'

Robert Louis Stevenson

'The cosiest and warmest corner of the most comfortable hearth is merely acceptable to the cat.'

George Robey

'All other animals when they sleep lie in attitudes of prostration and fatigue. To the cat alone has Nature vouchsafe the privilege of such sleep as the poets, without doing too great a violence to reality, might describe as meditation and reverie.'

Marius Vachon

'It is now possible to feed your cat on salmon flakes in lobster jelly or a delicious turkey paté which would not look out of place on a smart dinner table.'

Joan Smith

'When I tire of cows' milk...I am supplied with goats' or giraffes' or any other kind I desire. Once, when I was ill and cranky I refused to eat the nice, tender grey mouse that was served me in bed and insisted that I would not taste anything but a green mouse with lavender stripes....I mention these things to give you an idea of the life of a pussycat princess. It is a life of splendour and ease. One can have anything at all.'

Edward Anthony

'No other animal in creation can boast of having inspired so many superior minds.'

Marius Vachon

'Prose books are the show dogs I breed and sell to support my cat.'

Robert Graves

'Nobody is completely impervious to cats.'

Cassandra (William Connor)

'A home without a cat, and well-fed, well-petted and properly revered cat, may be a perfect home, perhaps, but how can it prove it?'

Mark Twain

'Cats, incidentally, are a great warm-up for a successful marriage – they teach you your place in the household.'

Paul Gallico

'How you behave towards cats here below determines your status in Heaven.'

Robert A.Heinlein

'It is not well with us who love to have the most companionable of all beasts near to us for sympathy. They go but a little way with us and then leave us. It is not good for us to measure life by the deaths of so many friends.'

Oswald Barron

'It is perhaps easier for a cat to train a man than for a man to train a cat. A cat who desires to live with human beings makes it his business to see that the so-called superior race behaves in the proper manner towards him.'

Carl Van Lechten

'They say the test of literary prowess is whether a man can write an inscription. I say: 'Can he name a kitten?''

Samuel Butler

Romantic tails

Chapter Ten

Common Cat Superstitions

In my book *The Cat Basket* I included a list of 10 common superstitions relating to cats. I thought I'd pretty much covered the territory. But the readers of that book have been kind enough to send me an astonishing number of superstitions I omitted from my original list. So, here are another 21 common superstitions relating to cats. The country from which each superstition originated is given in brackets. (Please do not follow any of the appalling medical advice contained in these superstitions.)

1. 'If you swallow a cat's hair, you won't get to heaven.' (America)

2. 'It's bad luck to step on a cat.' (England)

3. 'It's good luck if a stray cat follows you home.' (England)

4. 'When cats are playful a storm is coming.' (China)

5. 'The sleeping cat does not catch a mouse.' (Spain. Judging by the number of sleeping cats to be seen in Spain the mice must have a pretty carefree time.)

6. 'Let the cat into the house first when moving to a new home.' (England)

7. 'It is bad luck to let crumbs fall on a cat.' (England)

8. 'If you want to grow a beard, let a cat lick cream off your face.' (America)

9. 'It's lucky to have a cat in the theatre.' (England. But another superstition rules that it is unlucky for a cat to walk across stage during a performance.)

10. 'To cure shingles, get three drops of blood from the end of a black cat's tail and apply it to the shingles.' (Scotland)

11. 'To heal a sore, let the cat lick it.' (Wales)

12. 'To stop the bleeding from a cut or injury, keep repeating the words 'white cat' until the bleeding stops or you pass out.' (Scotland)

13. 'To cure the blues, swing a dead cat round your head three times by the tail.' (Wales)

14. 'To cure rheumatism, put a cat's pelt on the affected area.' (England)

15. 'To prevent rheumatism hold a cat in your lap.' (Holland)

16. 'People who have delusions and wild fantasies can be cured if they become friendly with a cat.' (Scotland)

17. 'If you dream about a cat which bites you then you have an enemy whom you thought was a friend.' (England)

18. 'Whoever cares well for cats will marry as happily as he/she could wish.' (France)

19. 'It is bad luck to go into a burning house and rescue the people before the cat.' (England)

20. 'If a girl treads on a cat's tail, she will not find a husband before a year is out. (France)

21. 'If a cat comes to your house, welcome it. If you send a cat away you will get bad luck.' (England)

Chapter Eleven

How Much Have You Learned From Your Cat?

Answer these questions to find out how successful your cat has been in teaching you how to behave.

1. Which of these is most important for successful mouse hunting:
a)   speed
b)   patience
c)   gloves

2. If you did catch a mouse what you would you do with it:
a)   play with it for a while, eviscerate it and then eat it
b)   scream, let the mouse go and jump up onto a chair

3. If a relative or friend offers you food that doesn't taste very good, do you:
a)   eat it and say how much you enjoyed it
b)   eat it and say nothing
c)   leave it and walk away
d)   leave it, go outside and catch yourself a mouse which you bring into the house and eat very noisily

4. You do something embarrassing (such as break a vase) do you:
a)   apologise profusely (and, in the case of the vase, offer to buy the owner a replacement)
b)   turn away, pretend it has nothing to do with you, and lick your bottom

5. You spot a magazine. Do you:

a)   read it

b)   sit on it

6. The neighbours buy a dog. Do you:

a)   pat it, say hello to it and say what a nice looking animal it is

b)   sit on the fence, just out of reach and drive it crazy

7. You sit so close to the fire that you begin to burn. Do you:

a)   jump up, panic, scream and pat at the burning area

b)   stay asleep and let someone else move you away from the fire

8. You have been outside in the garden and your feet are very muddy. Do you:

a)   tread carefully to avoid getting mud on the carpet

b)   head straight for the thickest, softest carpet because you know the mud will transfer from your feet quickly when you walk on a soft carpet

9. A mouse goes under the wardrobe and stays there. Do you

a)   spend three days waiting for it to come out and then, when your waiting is unrewarded, empty the wardrobe, hire two men to move it and watch in dismay as the mouse dives under the bed

b)   sit and wait for an hour and then go for a stroll in the garden and forget about the mouse

10. If you climbed a tree would you:

a)   work out beforehand how you were going to get down

b)   just worry about going up, in the knowledge that when you want to come down you can call for help and be rescued by a man on a ladder

11. Where do you put things you don't want:

a)   in the rubbish bin

b)   under the fridge

12. If someone calls you and you are busy do you:
a)   ignore them completely until you're ready and can spare the time
b)   stop what you're doing and rush to see what they want

Now check your score:

1. a) 3 b) 3 c) 1
2. a) 3 b)1
3. a) 1 b) 2 c) 3 d) 4
4. a) 1 b) 3
5. a) 1 b) 3
6. a) 1 b) 3
7. a) 1 b) 3
8. a) 1 b) 3
9. a) 1 b) 3
10. a) 1 b) 3
11. a) 1 b) 3
12. a) 3 b) 1

What do your results mean?
If you scored 15 or less then I'm afraid that you haven't learn much from your cat. This is not, of course, the cat's fault. (In an ideal world – and as far as cats are concerned that's what we live in – nothing is ever the cat's fault.) If you have failed to learn what your cat has tried to teach you then it is, I'm afraid, entirely your fault. You need to concentrate more and try harder.

If you scored 16 to 24 you are coming along nicely and should be able to award yourself a set of whiskers in just a few months' time.

If you scored 25 or more you can feel well-catisfied with yourself. You are an excellent pupil and can think of yourself as an honorary cat. Thank the cat and buy it a new toy and a case of its favourite food.

Chapter Twelve

Word Games For Cat Lovers

By changing just one letter at a time it is possible to change the word 'cat' into the word 'fur' in just three moves. For example::

cat --- car --- cur --- fur

Each time a letter is changed a new word is produced.

Now, using the same technique, changing one letter at a time and producing a new word every time you do so, try to:

- change the word 'fur' to the word 'ear' in two moves
- change the word 'milk' to the word 'mice' in two moves
- change the word 'kitten' to the word 'litter' in three moves
- change the word 'wool' to the word 'ball' in four moves
- change the word 'cat' to the word 'lap' in two moves
- change the word 'pet' to the word 'paw' in two moves
- change the word 'dog' to the word 'cat' in three moves
- change the word 'nap' to the word 'tom' in three moves
- change the word 'purr' to the word 'bird' in five moves
- change the word 'basket' to the word 'washes' in six moves
- change the word 'puss' to the word 'boot' in six moves
- change the word 'fish' to the word 'food' in six moves
- change the word 'puss' to the word 'mice' in seven moves
- change the word 'white' to the word 'black' in nine moves

Within moments Tiddles discovered that the old saying "Look before you leap" contained more good sense than he had previously thought.

Answers:

- fur to ear: fur, far, ear

- milk to mice: milk, mile, mice

- kitten to litter: kitten, bitten, bitter, litter

- wool to ball: wool, tool, toll, tall, ball

- cat to lap: cat, cap, lap

- pet to paw: pet, pat, paw

- dog to cat: dog, cog, cot, cat

- nap to tom: nap, tap, top, tom

- purr to bird: purr, burr, burn, barn, bard, bird

- basket to washes: basket, basked, masked, mashed, dashed, dashes, washes

- puss to boot: puss, pass, past, post, cost, coot, boot

- fish to food: fish, fist, list, lost, loot, foot, food

- puss to mice: puss, pass, past, pact, pace, lace, lice, mice

- white to black: white, write, trite, trice, trick, brick, crick, crack, clack, black

Chapter Thirteen

Uprights And Their Cats

1. The Proud Parents

Richard and Lucinda Todmorton, who are both in their 40's, married late and have no children. They do, however, have a cat called Heidi, whom they both adore. Richard is a solicitor and until recently Lucinda worked as an estate agent. She retired early, giving up a responsible and promising position as a senior adviser, in order to spend more time at home with Heidi. 'It's no exaggeration to say that our lives

Our lives revolve around our cat

revolve around our cat,' admits Lucinda, with a girlish blush. 'We both love her very much.' She pauses. 'We couldn't love a daughter more,' she admits. Richard and Lucinda haven't had a holiday for three years because they can't bear to leave Heidi with anyone. 'We did once go away for a night but we had a sleepless night, got up at 5.30 am and drove back home. Heidi was fast asleep on our bed when we got there. We didn't even think she'd noticed that we'd gone. We were very relieved.'

2. The Show Off

'I've always shown all my cats,' says Enid Higginbottom. 'I really think they enjoy it just as much as I do. In fact, if the truth be known, I really do it for them. They love being made a fuss of and seeing all their little furry friends.' Enid has three cats, two Siamese (one called Prince Alfred de Fouttoncourt III, the other called Prince Edward George) and a Persian (called Lady Antonia Younghusband), and over the 17 years she's been showing her cats Miss Higginbottom has accumulated an impressive array of silver cups and rosettes. A large, glass-fronted cupboard in the living room is filled with her collection

"The shampooing is the most important part of the preparation"

of trophies. 'I start getting the cats ready a fortnight before a show,' she says. 'The shampooing is the most important part of the preparation and I always do the Persian three or four times in the week before a show. At first she hated being shampooed but these days she really loves it. I think it's because she knows that she's going to be on display again. She's very vain, of course. But then most cats are, aren't they?'

3. The Farmer

Jim Lacklustre isn't quite sure how many cats live on his farm. 'I've got 127 cows, 346 sheep and 24 pigs, but I've never stopped to count the cats,' he says, when asked. 'It's difficult anyway,' he adds. 'There always seem to be new ones around.' When asked why he doesn't know the number he looks confused, as though he's been asked something entirely unreasonable. 'Why would I?' he asks, clearly puzzled. The cats on Jim's farm live in his four large and rather ramshackle barns and feed themselves on mice and other rodents. They are close to being feral. 'We found the body of one cat under a bale of straw,' says Jim, trying to think of something interesting to say about his cats. 'The bale must have fallen on it. Squashed flat and mummified it was.' When asked if he ever feeds the cats Jim's confusion grows. 'Why should I feed 'em?' he asks, genuinely bewildered. 'They get all the vermin they can eat.' Jim's attitude may seem uncaring to some but to him it's just business. 'You can't milk them, there's no market for cat fur and there's more decent meat on a

chicken than there is on a cat,' he says, explaining why he has little interest in animals which cannot contribute to the bottom line. When asked if he ever gives names to any of his cats he looks puzzled. 'Why would I do that?' he asks.

4. The Cat Woman

Elsie Wrigglesworth lives alone in the two-bedroomed cottage where she was born 73 years ago. She may not have any human companionship but she cannot truly be said to be alone since she shares her home with 76 cats. She knows all their names.

'Since I was 22 I've always had more cats than my age,' she says proudly. She lost her fiancé in the Second World War (he was killed at Dunkirk) and until her 55th birthday worked as a librarian. She took early retirement to look after her cats and now acquires new cats like a modern politician's wife collects shoes and handbags. 'I've got a lot of love to give,' she says. 'And I need to give it away. Cats are wonderful for soaking up love. I don't care whether they love me back or not. Giving love can be just as fulfilling as receiving it.' She knows the names and personalities of all her cats. 'That one is called Chatterbox,' she says, pointing to a black and white cat with a slightly wonky ear. 'She makes more noise than all others put together.' She laughs merrily at something she's just remembered. 'When she had a cold and lost her voice for a few days a friend of mine who helps me feed them said it was a case of no mews is good mews.' On the day of our visit Miss Wrigglesworth acquired two cats who had been abandoned by a neighbour who had emigrated to Spain. The cats had been brought round by the new owner of the house who said she was allergic to cats and didn't like having them around. Miss Wrigglesworth's cats all have names. She has named the two most recent additions to her household Sherlock and Mycroft.

5. The Academics

'I've been keen on cats ever since I read about Charles Dickens and the affection he had for his cat Wilhemina,' says Professor Hodge-Willborough-D'Eath, the author of *A Concise History Of Macedonian Economic History* and *A Second Concise History Of Macedonian Economic History*. The Professor was just six years old at the time and had already decided that he was going to be an author. 'I persuaded my parents to buy me a cat for Christmas,' he remembers. 'And I've kept cats ever since.' Professor Hodge-Willborough-D'Eath is married to Pamela ffanshaw-Sykies, the noted feminist and star panellist on the television show *Whose Bosom Is It Anyway?* They have a mackerel tabby and a tortoiseshell called Chairman Miaow. ('The cat doesn't believe in the principle of ownership,' explains the Professor. 'He insists on sleeping on my bed and he would steal my dinner if given half a chance.') Sadly, Ms ffanshaw-Sykies does not share her husband's affection for animals and the Professor's current feline companions, the gloriously named Archbishop Lewis Dodgson and Chairman Miaow, are only allowed into the couple's showpiece Victorian home (twice featured on the television show *Celebrity Homes We Would Like To Own*) if accompanied by an alert member of the couple's domestic staff (made up of an ever-changing supply of students from Macedonia who are earning their way through college) under instructions to make sure

"I persuaded my parents to buy me a cat for Christmas."

Shane, and his white Persian cat, Barbra.

that if a cat shows any signs of anti-social behaviour it is picked up and whisked away immediately.

6. The Entertainer

Shane Dale admits to being 49, though there are some in 'the business' who have been known to suggest that it has taken him an unusually long time to get through his forties. Those who hold this theory feel that their suspicions are vindicated by the fact that Shane celebrated his 40th birthday (in some style) in 1985. Home for Shane is a now luxury sea view apartment on the South Coast which the star shares with his long time manager and 'best friend' Freddie, and their white Persian cat Lady Barbra. Whenever Shane is photographed he always insists that he is pictured in at least one shot with Lady Barbra perched on his knees. The cat is now as much a part of Shane's show business image as his now very slightly old-fashioned heavily frilled sky blue shirt (worn open to the still muscular waist) and the round-the-year tan (slightly too orange to be natural). Shane's early years were spent working in what he now likes to call 'speciality' clubs (though he is more reticent about describing the 'speciality') and his big break came when an early appearance on a television variety programme was given extra publicity after the fortuitous kidnapping of Lady Barbra. The nation held its breath for seven days until Lady Barbra was mysteriously returned to her owner and all ended happily. No one was ever questioned, let alone arrested, in connection with the case. It is a well-kept secret that the original Lady Barbra died some years ago and was replaced. The current Lady Barbra is believed by some in the cat trade to be the fourth Persian to have borne that name.

7. The High Fliers

The Robinsons do not regard themselves as wealthy, though they have three homes. 'We live right on the financial edge,' insists Fiona. 'It's pretty much a hand-to-mouth existence.' Her husband Nigel is a banker, as was she before she 'retired' to become a full-time mother and housewife. Their main home is a town house in Chelsea. They spend weekends in their eight-bedroomed cottage in the Cotswolds. Last year, they used Nigel's annual bonus to purchase outright a chalet in the Swiss Alps, where they like to go skiing. The Robinsons have four children (Henry, Charles, Prunella and Rosie) and employ a full-time nanny and several other members of staff. Their household is completed by two Dalmatians and four cats. The Dalmatians go with the family wherever it goes but two of the cats live in their Chelsea home and two live in the cottage in the Cotswolds. All four cats are Siamese. 'We don't move the cats about,' says Fiona. 'I think cats need a stable

Animals help make a house complete, as long as they're the right colours.

background.' The male cats are all called Mr Felix and the female cats are Ms Feline. The children add numbers to these names to distinguish between cats; so there is, for example, a Mr Felix 1 and a Mr Felix 2. At the moment the Robinsons don't have any cats at their home in

Switzerland but Fiona says that when they've found permanent live-in staff for the chalet they will acquire a pair of Siamese to keep out there. 'Animals help make a house complete,' says Mrs Robinson. 'As long as they're the right colours and don't scratch the furniture, of course.'

8. The Salesman's Wife

'There's usually a cat around here somewhere,' says Annie Oliphant, peering around the kitchen. She has a towel over one arm and a smudge of baking powder on her nose. She looks harassed and talks very quickly as though accustomed to having her listeners walk out on her. 'We used to have just the one – called Tiffany – but although the people we got her from said she'd been 'done' she obviously hadn't because she'd been living with us for less than a year when she presented us with five kittens. My husband Dave is a salesman and he's away more than he's here so I wanted to find homes for three or four of the kittens but the children wanted to keep them and on one of his rare visits back home my husband sided with them so in the end we kept them though of

"I have little conversations with any cat."

167

course it's me who looks after them; not that I mind in the slightest but I do sometimes wish that Dave or one of the children would help with the litter tray. Having said that I have to admit that I did get some help with the tray when I was pregnant with Jade, that's our youngest. Dave was worried that I might get toxoplasmosis so he made Kevin, our oldest boy, help me. Mind you, if I'm honest he didn't do much. He's 15 and he's hardly ever here so if I'd left it to him the cat's tray wouldn't have been emptied more than once a week – if that. So I ended up doing it myself and paying him £5 a week for nothing.' Despite the fact that the cats add to her already back-breaking workload Annie is very fond of the cats. 'They're great company,' she says. 'I find myself talking to them during the day. I have little conversations with them. It may sound strange but I would be very lonely without the cats. But I don't tell anyone I talk to them. I'd be so embarrassed if people found out.'

9. The Boy

David and his cat Timmy are 'best pals'. 'They're inseparable,' says David's mother. 'Except for when David has to go to school they are always together. On school days Timmy will often walk the quarter mile to the school gate and wait for

his young master outside the school gate.' 'He came right into the school once,' says David proudly. 'He appeared in the assembly hall when we were having morning non-religious prayers. My class teacher made me take him back home and lock him in my bedroom.' 'It was all very embarrassing,' says David's mother, though David himself doesn't seem to be in the slightest bit embarrassed by what happened. 'Timmy is the cleverest cat in the whole wide world,' insists David who claims his cat can walk on his hind legs. 'I have to hold his front paws,' he admits. 'But with a bit more practice I absolutely know that he'll be able to walk on his hind legs by himself.'

10. The Widow

'I'd always wanted a cat,' says Mrs Highsmith, a well-preserved 60-something widow who lives alone in the bungalow she and her late husband had bought for their retirement. 'We thought we were very clever,' remembers Mrs Highsmith. 'Graham, my late husband, reckoned that if we bought the bungalow while we could still get around we would be able to arrange it just how we wanted it, and get nicely settled in.' She sighs. 'Then he upped and died. On minute he was putting up a new pelmet in the spare bedroom and the next minute I was coming home from the funeral to an empty house and having to get an odd job man in to finish the pelmet.' Mr Highsmith had refused to have a cat in the house – he   insisted

"She's a very understanding and forgiving cat."

they made him feel uncomfortable – but with him gone Mrs Highsmith wasted no time in finding a feline companion with whom to share what she calls her 'bungalow years'. 'Catarina Sarah-Louise is the best friend I've ever had,' says Mrs Highsmith, stroking the tortoiseshell cat with whom she now shares her life. 'I got a tortoiseshell because a friend told me that they're the most loving of all cats.' Catarina Sarah-Louise looks up and Mrs Highsmith tickles her under the chin. 'She likes that,' whispers Mrs Highsmith as though sharing a secret discovery. 'Catarina Sarah-Louise has given me a new reason for living. I can talk to her in a way I could never talk to Graham. She's a very understanding and forgiving cat.'

11. The High Fliers

'We bought our cat Princess Esmerelda Middlemarsh Ffanshaw-Blythe the III from a specialist breeder in the North of England,' says Fiona. 'We found the company on the Internet after putting 'very expensive cats' into a search engine. The cats they sell are the most expensive in the world and Princess Esmerelda was the most expensive cat they had available when we e-mailed.

They sent her down to us by courier in an expensive hand-made cat carrier made by Peruvian peasants. She's short-haired and white, of course. A long-haired cat would moult and any colour would clash with our furnishings. We have a veterinary assistant in twice a day to feed her and clear out her litter tray of course. She also bleaches the little black patch underneath Princess Esmeralda's chin.' When asked what they call her when trying to get her back into the apartment Fiona seems genuinely surprised. 'Oh we wouldn't let her out,' she says. 'She's far too expensive for that. The insurance company wouldn't allow it. Besides, calling her name would take far too long and the veterinary assistant goes home at 5.30pm.

12. The Conflicted

Gordon and Lydia met at a party and have been living together for 18 months now. They share an elegant three-bedroom terraced home with Gordon's cat Jemima and Lydia's cat Pippa. Sadly, the two cats do not get on as well as the two Uprights and in order to prevent the two cats attempting to kill one another, Gordon and Lydia have had

to divide their home into two quite separate parts. Jemima lives upstairs, having her little tray in the bathroom and her food and water bowls in the spare bedroom. Pippa lives downstairs with her litter tray in the utility room and her comestibles in the kitchen. Jemima is allowed out for exercise from 9 am until 1 pm while Pippa takes her exercise from 2 pm until 6 pm. The doors into the hall are kept closed and an additional door has been installed at the top of the stairs, effectively turning the downstairs hall and the stairs into a no-buffer zone between the two halves of the house. 'It works quite well,' claims Gordon. 'The alternative would, of course, have been Lydia and I splitting up.'

Chapter Fourteen

Pomes About Cats

Thank You, God For Making Kittens

The very best thing about kittens is not that they are soft, cuddly
and adorable,
It is not that they are heart-stoppingly beautiful,
It is not that they are trusting and without care.
It is simply that they grow up to be cats.
That'll do.
Thank you God for that.

Catcher In The Park

A well-groomed cat from the city
Who was charming, cuddly and pretty
Rose with the lark
To catch mice in the park.
Why not, she enquired, I'm a Kitty.

"Never mind," said Tiddles. "I lost my first mouse too. In fact I lost my first eight mice," he lied.

"Did you really?" said Snuggles, instantly feeling a good deal better.

A Loyal Son

A tall and handsome young male
Travelled home through sleet and through hail.
He said: 'I may be a Tom
But I still love my Mom,
So I visit each week without fail.'

Different Views

A man and a cat, good friends and true
Went off to the hills 'cus they quite liked the view
Together they climbed an old gnarled tree
And looked quite hard 'til they saw the sea
I'm puzzled, said the man, cus the sea is blue
And I don't know why. I haven't a clue.
I don't give a jot, purred the cat with glee
I'm just happy 'cus you're here with me.

Dottie

Lovely wee Dottie confessed she was bitten
By love for a gorgeous, delightful small kitten
'I've loved cats a lot
Since I was a tot
But by this one I'm totally smitten.'

Muddy Paws

Cats who live in the city
Always think that a kitty
Who has mud on a paw
Is bound by some law
To never be thought of as pretty.

Up A Tree

A cat with fur long and soft
Spent a lot of her time up aloft
She once caught a flea
After climbing a tree
And promised thereafter to stop.

Happy Purrthday

Another year older
Another year of joy
Another year of memories
Another year's gift from God
How do you say 'thank you'
For such a present?

Nothing

Nothing can move quite as fast as a cat
And nothing can sit quite as still.
One moment the cat will be all at peace
Fast asleep, far away from the world.
But then, in an instant,
Before you can blink,
He'll be up and about in a whirl.
Nothing can move quite as fast as a cat
And nothing can sit quite as still.

Without A Cat

Without a cat
I am like
A boat without a rudder
A cloud without a breeze
A tree without a leaf
A library without a book
A flower without a petal
A house without a roof
A car without an engine
But with a cat
I am like
A warm sunny day on the beach.

What Is It About Cats?

What is it about Timmy that I remember most?
Is it the way I used to comb his long grey fur to prevent it
knotting?
Is it the way he always moved around the house to find a patch
of sunshine?
Or is it the way he used to follow me when I went to school,
walking along beside me as I tried (half-heartedly) to persuade him
to go back?

"I think it must be a humming bird," said Tiddles

What is it about Dick that I remember most?
Is it the way he used to drop a marble into my slipper when he
heard me arrive at the front door, so that I would be reminded to
play with him?
Is it the way he would sit on my neck licking at my scalp with
his sandpaper tongue?
Is it the way he would sit on top of the television trying to catch
the snooker balls?

What is it about Harry that I remember most?
Is it the way he tried to teach Alice and Thomasina how to hunt?
Is it the way he could jump six feet into the air and land on top
of the garden fence?
Is it the way he could go up a tree without a pause?

What is it about Alice that I remember most?
Is it the way that she would come running towards me, tail up
straight, when she saw me returning home?
Is it the way she waded through a stream because I was standing
on the other side?
Is it the way she would leap from the floor to my shoulders while
I was having a shave?

What is it about Thomasina that I remember most?
Is it the way she would walk across the fields with me?
Is it the way she would sleep on my computer keyboard, typing
out secret, coded messages as she moved to get comfortable?
Is it the way she loved to sleep on the windowsill in my study?

Cats are all memorable in so many different ways
But the one thing that I remember about them all
Is that I loved them
(I think they loved me too. But that really doesn't matter.)

The Twelve-Year-Old Kitten
(When does a kitten become a cat?)

A kitten loves to chase its tail.
So does a cat.
A kitten loves to climb (curtains or trees will do).
So does a cat.
A kitten likes to sleep.
So does a cat.
A kitten looks adorable and innocent when asleep.
So does a cat.
A kitten loves to play.
So does a cat.
A kitten jumps from a chair with a non-existent crash.
(Making a noise like an early autumn leaf landing on the grass.)
So does a cat.
A kitten never looks guilty.
Nor does a cat.
All things considered,
We have a kitten
Who will be twelve next month.
And there's the truth.
There are no cats.
At heart, they're all still kittens.

Spreading Less Over More

We all live over-hectic lives
We cram more and more into the same amount of time
Has it ever occurred to you that if cats have a practical function
(And it embarrasses me to suggest that this might be so)
It could simply be to show us how to have a more fulfilling life
By choosing what we do more carefully,
Concentrating on those things we choose to do
And giving them our full attention.

And Finally...

Paws For Thought

You haven't paid for this bit of the book. It's a present from me to you. It isn't an outside advertisement or an appeal of any kind. I'm not asking you to give money. All I want you to do is to read the next few pages. I'm paying for the paper and the ink. This bit of the book doesn't even appear on the contents list. All you have to give is a few minutes of your time.

Since you've got this far in the book it is a fair guess that you like cats. And, as you've probably guessed, I do too. But I wonder if you know just what terrible things are being done to cats in your name – and, very often, with your money.

★ ★ ★

Most people don't eat cats and so cats aren't farmed for food. Not many people wear clothes made from cat fur and so there aren't many cat fur farms.

But vivisectors do like cats. And they like tame, quiet cats best of all. Some cats are bred especially for laboratory work. Others are stolen from gardens and suburban streets.

(A vivisector once explained that he and his colleagues prefer tame domestic cats because they tend to be more trusting and less troublesome when being handled in the laboratory. It is for this reason that so many domestic cats go missing every year. Thousands are kidnapped (perhaps this should be 'catnapped') by professional cat thieves and sold to vivisectors so that they can be used in laboratories where animal experiments are performed.)

Vivisectors do terrible things to cats. Most of us don't like to think about the hideously barbaric experiments which are conducted behind locked doors but, even though I have been campaigning against vivisection for years, even I am sometimes horrified and sickened by what goes on.

In one experiment, for example, researchers reported that they had sewn up the eyes of young kittens. In another experiment a researcher drilled holes into the skulls of cats and then poured chemicals into and around the cats' brains – without giving the cats any anaesthesia. The experiment consisted of writing down, in precise and cold-blooded detail, the way the cats suffered; squirming and screaming to the very end. As a doctor I've seen some pretty awful things. But I simply don't understand how any sentient human being could perform experiments of this type.

★ ★ ★

Those who support vivisection often (but not always) do so on the grounds that animal experiments are essential for medical progress. Some vivisectors and vivisection supporters claim that research on animals is justified because it expands our range of knowledge. Just 'seeing what happens' is, they say, all the reason they need. But many vivisectors (and probably most of the crafty ones) claim that experiments on cats, kittens, dogs, puppies and other animals are an essential part of medical research. 'Without such experiments,' they claim, 'there will be no progress in the wars on cancer, heart disease and other deadly illnesses.'

Millions of people accept this argument. With varying degrees of reluctance they claim that if experiments on cats (and other animals) can save human lives, or reduce human suffering, then those experiments must be accepted as an unpleasant but necessary price we have to pay.

As it happens I don't accept this argument. I don't accept that the end – however barbaric – can justify the means. I don't believe that progress obtained through cold-blooded, outrageous cruelty is progress worth having.

But whether or not I accept the argument is irrelevant.

Because the simple truth is that experiments on cats (and other animals) are unpredictable, unreliable and utterly worthless. Laboratory experiments on animals are of absolutely no value whatsoever to doctors or patients.

That's not a point of view. It's a fact of life. No one who has studied the facts can dispute it. Animal experiments are performed not to help people, not to save human lives, but because they are an essential part of a multi-billion pound industry.

★ ★ ★

I have long been opposed to the use of live animals in laboratory experiments. I am opposed to this practice for several reasons. I believe that the use of live, sentient creatures in this way is barbaric, unnecessary and immoral. And I believe that it is the reliance of drug companies on animal experiments which is largely responsible for the current epidemic of iatrogenesis – diseases caused, in general, by doctors and, in particular, by prescription drugs.

I can prove the accuracy of what I say in several quite simple ways.

★ ★ ★

First, many of the drugs which doctors prescribe for human patients are known to cause cancer or other serious problems when given to animals. I can give you the names of dozens of drugs which, when they were initially tested on animals, were shown to cause cancer or other serious health problems. (A fairly extensive list is available on my website www.vernoncoleman.com)

Here's how it works: if a drug is given to an animal and the animal dies (or is made ill) the results of the test will be ignored. The drug will still be given to people on the grounds that people are different to animals and so the results of the tests on animals can be ignored. If, on the other hand, a drug is given to an animal, and the animal survives the experience, the drug company and its researchers will claim that this shows the drug to be safe.

The Government's advisers collude with this nonsense.

Nothing illustrates the nonsense of animal testing better than this. When the results of animal tests are commercially inconvenient they are ignored as irrelevant!

Drug companies, the medical establishment and the Government must know that animal experiments are worthless. They defend the fiction – that animal experiments are of value – because of the vast financial benefits to the drugs industry.

The killer question (which vivisectors and their supporters can never answer) is: Why test on animals if you're going to ignore the results when they are inconvenient?

The truth is simple.

Vivisection is so unreliable and unpredictable that the results can be ignored when they're inconvenient. And that's why they do it.

★ ★ ★

Second, even the most enthusiastic vivisectors will admit that some of the experiments done on animals are grossly misleading and worthless. Moreover, they will also admit that they don't know which animal experiments are likely to produce accurate answers and which will produce misleading answers.

But surely, if you don't know which experiments are useful – and which are misleading – then *all* animal experiments must be useless.

★ ★ ★

The supporters of vivisection frequently claim that doctors approve of animal experiments. This is, quite simply, not true.

When I conducted the largest ever survey of doctors (over 650 doctors were questioned) I got the following results:

♦ 88% of doctors agreed that laboratory experiments performed on animals can be misleading because of anatomical and physiological differences between animals and humans.

♦ 69% of doctors agreed that too many experiments on animals are performed.

♦ 51% of doctors agreed that patients would suffer fewer side effects if new drugs were tested more extensively on human cell and tissue cultures.

♦ 81% of doctors said they would like to see scientists trying harder to find alternatives to animals for testing drugs and cosmetics.'

★ ★ ★

Third, after I gave evidence to the House of Lords Animals in Scientific Procedures Committee (at the Committee's invitation), the Committee wrote asking me to review papers which had been submitted by the Department of Health in an attempt to substantiate the Government's argument that animal testing is both necessary and efficacious.

The report which follows is a precis of the report which I sent to the Committee. My report clearly established that none of the papers submitted proved that animal testing is either necessary or efficacious.

Summary of Conclusions by Dr Vernon Coleman

On the basis of this evidence, and assuming that this is the best scientific evidence that the Department of Health can find in support of its argument that toxicological testing on animals is of value, then, assuming that the Committee intends to base its conclusions on sound scientific evidence, the Committee has no choice but to at the very least call for an independent inquiry (for example a Royal Commission) into the relevance of animal experimentation.

These papers do not substantiate the claims made by the Government. Indeed, on the contrary, the evidence available here proves my point: animal experimentation is unpredictable, unreliable and of no value whatsoever to human beings. I would be happy to appear before the Committee again if the Committee has any questions based on my analysis of these papers. I would also be happy to appear before the Committee and debate with any expert witness provided by the Department of Health.

These papers do not prove the value of animal experiments. On the contrary they clearly prove that animal experimentation is so unpredictable and unreliable that it is worthless to human beings.

I can understand why drug companies support vivisection: it is a double-edged tool which enables them to sell drugs for a mass market without the inconvenience of performing tests which might prove that a potentially profitable drug causes dangerous side effects and cannot therefore be marketed. If a test on animals shows that a drug causes cancer the test will be ignored on the grounds that animals are different to people. If a test on animals shows that a drug does not cause cancer the results of the test will be used to help substantiate the claim that the drug is safe for humans. Drug companies just cannot lose when performing animal tests. The Committee will be aware that I submitted a list of 50 drugs which are currently prescribed for human beings but which are known to cause cancer or other serious health problems in animals. These adverse results are all ignored on the grounds that animals are different to people – proving quite conclusively that initial toxicology testing on animals is utterly pointless.

I am perfectly happy to accept that animal testing is more expensive than other forms of testing.

But the evidence supports the view that drug companies perform animal tests because, although they may be more expensive than more effective forms of testing, they enable them to mass-market new drugs without the risk of having to withdraw potentially profitable products in the early stages.

The big question is: 'Why does the Government continue to support vivisection when the Department of Health cannot provide one jot of evidence in support of its claim that animal experimentation is valid and of value? Indeed, on the contrary, the evidence supplied by the Department of Health proves my argument much more effectively than it proves their argument.'

Surely the Department of Health should devote itself to finding the truth, and protecting the interests of patients, rather than simply attempting (in vain) to protect the commercial interests of the pharmaceutical industry? Assessing animal experimentation alongside non-animal experimentation would be a good starting point.

Finally, I would like the Department of Health to explain why it allows doctors to prescribe a huge number of drugs which cause cancer in animals and yet, at the same time, considers animal experiment results essential for the granting of licences to drug companies.

If you are going to demand that drug companies perform animal tests, and then going to ignore the results of those tests when they are inconvenient, why do the tests in the first place?

Four out of ten patients in the UK suffer unpleasant, severe or fatal side effects after taking prescription drugs. The cost of all these side effects puts a great burden on the NHS. If animal tests were abandoned, and drugs were tested more effectively, the nation would be healthier and the demands on the NHS would be much lighter.

The Committee, the most important official inquiry into the use of animals in experiments for decades, reported its findings direct to the Government. No one in the Government took up my offer to meet with 'experts' from the Department of Health. My analysis of the scientific papers submitted by the Department of Health appears on my website: www.vernoncoleman.com

★ ★ ★

And fourthly and finally, the vivisection supporters have been quite unable to find one patient whose life had been saved by animal experiments.

A couple of years ago I offered to give £250,000 to the first vivisector or vivisection supporter who could find a patient whose life had been saved by animal experiments. The offer was widely and repeatedly publicised in the national press, in magazines and on the Internet. But not one person came forward to claim the £250,000. No vivisector, or vivisection supporter, could produce a patient whose life had been saved by vivisection.

I think it is safe to assume from this that even the vivisectors know that no lives have been saved as a result of animal experiments.

★ ★ ★

After I had defeated vivisectors in a series of public debates (some of them televised) the vivisectors simply decided to refuse to debate with me. For many years now television and radio producers who have tried to set up debates between vivisectors and myself have been told that if the debate is to go ahead then some other opponent must be found.

The power of the drug industry (and the politicians and the parts of the medical establishment now owned by the drug industry) is so great that national newspapers are no longer willing to publish anything which seriously and effectively questions the validity of animal experiments.

★ ★ ★

Thank you for reading these few extra pages. Now that I am banned from writing about vivisection in newspapers and magazines, and banned from discussing the issue on television and radio, I have a problem sharing the truth with readers. Adding this small section to this book seemed one way. If you would like to know more you will find everything you need in my three books *Fighting for Animals, Why Animal Experiments Must Stop* and *Animal Rights Human Wrongs* and on my website www.vernoncoleman.com

The pro-vivisection movement is rich and powerful and has succeeded in propagating the myth that animal experiments are essential and valuable. If you share my view that vivisection is unnecessary and immoral, and you want to help stop it, you can help by explaining to your friends that the scientific evidence shows that animal experiments are at best worthless and at worst dangerously misleading. Animal experiments kill people as well as animals. Give your friends this book to read or ask them to visit www.vernoncoleman.com and look at the articles on vivisection.

For a catalogue of Vernon Coleman's books
please write to:

Publishing House
Trinity Place
Barnstaple
Devon EX32 9HG
England

| Telephone | 01271 328892 |
| Fax | 01271 328768 |

Outside the UK:

| Telephone | +44 1271 328892 |
| Fax | +44 1271 328768 |

Or visit our website:

www.vernoncoleman.com